A
Painter's
KITCHEN

Georgia O'Keeffe making a salad at the Ghost Ranch. © 1962 by Todd Webb.
Courtesy Evans Gallery, Portland, Maine.

A

Painter's
KITCHEN

RECIPES *from the* KITCHEN *of*
GEORGIA O'KEEFFE

By Margaret Wood
With a New Foreword by Deborah Madison

Museum of New Mexico Press
Santa Fe

Contents

Steven in the Garden, 1980. Photograph by Myron Wood. Courtesy and © Pikes Peak Library District.

MAIN DISHES 57

BREADS, GRAINS, & CEREALS 75

DESSERTS 91

BEVERAGES 103

Acknowledgments

The author would like to thank David Barbero for his encouragement and advice; Richard Faller for his food photography in the original edition; Michael and Marianne O'Shaugnessy and the Red Crane Staff for their ongoing support; Lelord Kordel, the Hilltop Herb Farm, and Redco Corporation for their recipe permissions; The Rodale Herb Book as the primary source for herb information; Mary Grether, my mother June Wood, Ernesto Mayans, Leonor Webelman, Myron Wood, and many supportive family members and friends. Finally, an acknowledgment to all the women who prepared the food in Georgia O'Keeffe's kitchens.

Vines and Garden, 1980. Photograph by Myron Wood. Courtesy and © Pikes Peak Library District.

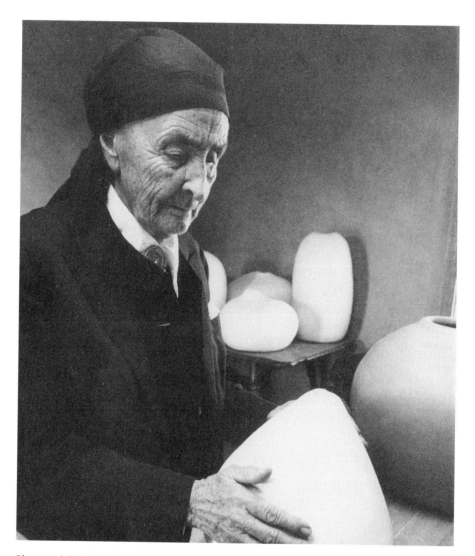

Photograph by Dan Budnick

Foreword

Deborah Madison

Like Margaret Wood, the author of *A Painter's Kitchen*, I too once lived—during the same years, in fact—as an assistant to an older woman. My older woman lived in a posh part of Long Island rather than rural New Mexico, and she was a writer, not a painter. Both women at times, even at the same time, lived in New York City. And both, we found, could be prickly, which is understandable given that we were young people trying to walk in their shoes and assume their well-worn routines. But Margaret and I agree that while it's kind of old-fashioned to live as an apprentice to a powerful older person, doing so gave us experiences that we both treasure today.

The kitchen side of my work led me into a world of Manhattans, cream soups, and canapés, the stylish urban foods of the fifties. This was a far cry from my own life as a cook in a Zen community where gardens and grain mills played an important role in our culinary lives, as they did for Georgia O'Keeffe.

A Painter's Kitchen is a book I deeply resonate with, but it's a deceptive one. It looks as if there's nothing special going on with the recipes, but read between the lines and everything that promises deep goodness is there, mainly the fruits of the garden translated with a sure hand into, say, a salad of torn herbs or a soup scented with lovage.

The hand is austere to be sure. No dish is encumbered with complicated embellishments; there are no intricate layerings of flavors and textures. Rather, the elemental minerality of garden vegetables stands solidly next to the warmth of grains, the occasional blunt meatiness of a steak, or the sweet-tart bite of an apple pie. And you just know that they are good dishes. There's nothing to mess them up. Absent are today's pet seasonings—the fennel pollen, the smoked salt or truffle oil. Oil is, in fact, just "oil."

Consider the minimal-sounding recipes. There's Kale. Spinach. Tomato Soufflé—one- or two-word titles that are a rarity among food writers today who feel they (we) must seduce the reader with promise right up front. But read carefully and you get the sense that O'Keeffe's dishes were the kind of simple foods that radiated the natural complexity of the very things we seek today—namely, food in its season, grown and handled with care. In addition to its peak flavor, there's a vitality that comes with garden food that takes the palette far beyond a nod to simplicity.

Read the recipes closely and you'll uncover some clues to their depth of flavor—the use of a mortar and pestle to grind the spices for that tomato soufflé; wheat ground fresh for the bread; an omelet studded with herbs from the garden; mashed potatoes infused with dandelion greens gathered in the spring. A tomato soup sports my favorite herb, the still seldom-seen lovage. Wild asparagus found growing on the irrigation ditches would have been sublime, as it is still today. A recipe for peas is as simple as can be, but consider that they were fresh peas. As the biodynamic gardener Alan Chadwick used to say, "The cooking has been done for you in the garden; it's merely finished in the kitchen." So imagine a bowl of peas, butter glistening as it slides over each green orb—hopefully you can do this—and you know this was eating at its best.

The Seed Savers Exchange was just starting when Margaret Wood was cooking in Miss O'Keeffe's kitchen. The exchange began the effort to connect people and their heritage seeds to one another, and today there are thousands of vegetable, herb, and flowers available, unique varieties that were nearly lost about the time O'Keeffe was tending her garden. These varieties all had names, often quite colorful and descriptive ones. While reading *A Painter's Kitchen* I found myself looking for traces of the old heirlooms. Indeed, there is the lovage mentioned above, and purple basil, which wasn't yet commonly known, but what were those apples that were so perfect for pie? They were yellow, they ripened in September—too late for the July Transparents—but what were they? A two-pound tomato is mentioned. Was it a Mortgage Lifter, or a freakily large Early Girl? I would love to know.

When I was first visiting Santa Fe and going to the Santa Fe Farmers' Market back in the late 1970s, I was struck by how uninteresting the produce seemed, with the exception of chiles and wild chokecherries. But at the same time I noticed how much better it tasted than food from the store. It was basic, but it was food grown in a garden. I suspect it was pretty much the same in the Abiquiu garden—simple garden vegetables picked daily. But it's when the eye goes to the details of garden and kitchen that the magic begins to occur.

Over tea one afternoon, I visited with Margaret Wood, who lives nearby in Santa Fe. She spoke about picking lettuces leaf by leaf to make a kind of "mesclun" or mix, one that preceded by decades the bags of "spring mix" we now so blithely reach for. And she spoke of salad as "the longest part of a meal," because she had to wash, then shake and pat dry on paper towels the greens, then cut the herbs by hand and tear the lettuce, also by hand. In discussing lettuce, Margaret tells me that she still gets a lot of pleasure out of experiencing the range of flavor held in a head of lettuce – how the tastes change from the outer to the inner leaves, from the tips to the stems—something she learned in the Abiquiu kitchen as a young woman.

O'Keeffe also had health on her mind, taking Adele Davis as one of her guides—hence the grinding of grain for flour for bread, or making yogurt using local goat's milk and a fine Swiss culture. People often express surprise that health and goodness can somehow be found together in the same food, but I take the point of view that goodness and healthfulness go hand in hand. Simple food, plucked from the earth and shaped with patience and care—does this offer goodness or health? I, for one, would hate to choose. I say it's the best of both. Or as O'Keeffe put it, "the spirit of fresh flavor and good health."

The recipes in *A Painter's Kitchen* are written by the woman who cooked them for O'Keeffe, who no doubt was watching over all. I especially enjoy Margaret Wood's recipe introductions and appreciate that they are not always about the dishes, which speak for themselves quite well. Often they are about the moment, a snippet of conversation between her and Miss O'Keeffe, guests who might have been there, the weather, where a meal might have been eaten. These are words that showcase the food and place it in its context. Not only are the recipe introductions a delight to read, they suggest that food is indeed a pleasurable part of a larger life, one that's woven around comings and goings, fireplaces and gardens, work and reflection—in short, something beyond just recipes. Together, the recipes and their context create the texture of a life, two lives really, that we are privileged to know.

Georgia O'Keeffe picking produce from her ranch garden (Abiquiu).
Photograph by John Loengard, *Life Magazine.* © 1968 by Time Warner, Inc.

Introduction

I met the painter Georgia O'Keeffe when she was ninety. I was twenty-four. She taught me how to cook simple, delicious food with many fresh ingredients when I worked as her companion from 1977 to 1982. I remember how she guided me through the large Abiquiu garden, telling me where all the vegetables, fruits, and herbs could be found. She spoke with pride about her organic produce: the two-pound tomato that was grown the previous summer, the tree that bore the best applesauce apples, and the hardy raspberries that survived one spring when all the other fruit froze.

The garden abundantly provided most of the produce for the O'Keeffe household. Miss O'Keeffe (as many of her acquaintances and the household staff called her) had planted this garden since the late 1940s when she had bought the Abiquiu house. At that time, the garden was in poor condition, the original structure was in ruins, and the property was used as a corral for pigs and cows. The house was completely remodeled, and the garden was reconditioned over a three-year period.

Miss O'Keeffe said that the garden was the main reason for buying the Abiquiu house; when she lived at Ghost Ranch, she had to go seventy miles over dirt roads to Santa Fe in search of fresh vegetables. So the large, rectangular garden area beside the house was gradually planted with vegetables, fruit trees, flowers, and herbs.

Garden preparation usually began in early March. Compost from the previous year was worked into the soil by the caretaker and gardener, who was in his seventies. His grandsons often helped with the work. Seeds were ordered by catalog, and "starters" were bought in a Santa Fe nursery. Miss O'Keeffe's business manager organized the planting according to the painter's specific advice. Originally, Miss O'Keeffe supervised the placement and planting of everything in the garden. She had definite ideas concerning dates and methods for planting each vegetable.

Early crops were planted in March so that the household could have radishes, lettuce, and spinach in May. Then, seeds for snow peas, chard, kale, carrots, turnips, beets, cucumbers, yellow and green squash, string beans, and corn were sown. Onion sets and garlic were planted next. Seedlings for several varieties of tomatoes, green chile, bell peppers, broccoli, and cabbage were put in last. Marigolds were strategically placed to repel unwanted insects.

Although vegetables received the largest space, the garden area was shared by herbs, flowers, trees, and bushes. Slightly uneven flagstone paths led between garden sections and over the irrigation canals. In a shady, somewhat overgrown area, herbs thrived: green and purple basil, lovage, marjoram, tarragon, dill, sorrel, chives, parsley, summer savory, and three kinds of mint. Nearby, grape hyacinths, crocuses, and daffodils were the first spring flowers to appear. Later, irises, lilacs, columbines, poppies, hollyhocks, and roses bloomed.

In the middle of the garden, near the long, brown adobe wall, was an immense mulberry tree. Pear trees grew along the wall to the west. Apple, apricot, and peach trees had been planted on a terrace to the east. A remarkably thick row of raspberry bushes was established behind the vegetables.

This large variety of plants was able to grow due to the abundance of water from nearby springs. The *acequia,* or ditch system, established centuries ago in New Mexico, provides spring water to the villagers on specified days and times of the week, according to their needs. The gardener diverted water from the main ditch two or three times weekly and guided the water through small canals throughout the garden area and the fruit tree terraces.

Much of the garden produce was dried, frozen, or canned for winter use. Apricots were dried on large screens in the open air. Bunches of herbs were hung to dry from the large round support beams, or vigas, in the pantry and

Indian Room. Green chile was roasted to remove the thin outer skin, then frozen. Quantities of corn were frozen, along with quelites (lamb's quarters) and green beans. Peaches, apricots, applesauce, and raspberries were frozen as well. Tomatoes, pickles, relishes, and fruit were canned in a variety of forms. Most food preservation was accomplished by the housekeeper, who generally prepared the principal meal of the day and performed a variety of other household tasks.

Miss O'Keeffe's staff bought the food that could not be grown in the garden. Organic grains and meats were preferred, when available. Miss O'Keeffe owned a small mill for stone-grinding her flour, and most of her bread was homemade. She bought eggs and local honey from various neighbors and

O'Keeffe Residence, 1960
(Abiquiu, the Indian Room)
by Laura Gilpin.
© 1981 Laura Gilpin
Collection, Amon Carter
Museum, Fort Worth, Texas.

Georgia O'Keeffe pouring tea at the Ghost Ranch.
© 1962 by Todd Webb. Courtesy Evans Gallery, Portland, Maine.

preferred to use herb salt rather than the commercial iodized variety. She cultivated a particular taste which focused on homegrown and natural foods.

Food served in the O'Keeffe household was always nutritious, tasty, and simply but beautifully presented. Miss O'Keeffe often wondered aloud, "Do you

Daffodils (Miss O'Keeffe's dining room, Abiquiu). © 1980 by Myron Wood.

think other people eat as well as we do?" In her nineties, she only occasionally ate in the homes of a few close friends and rarely dined out in restaurants. When she did dine elsewhere, she often remarked afterwards that it compared poorly with the food she was served in her own home.

O'Keeffe's Kitchen Sink, Ghost Ranch © 1975 by Dan Budnik.

Miss O'Keeffe exhibited discriminating taste in all elements of her surroundings, so it is not surprising that she was very particular about the food she ate and the environment in which it was prepared. Both her Abiquiu and Ghost Ranch kitchens were spacious areas with an abundance of supplies and several large windows.

The Abiquiu kitchen was a rather large, rectangular, white room with an intimate view of ornamental cherry trees and the distant Chama River Valley to the north. The largest appliance was a dependable Chambers gas stove from the late 1940s, with a stainless steel four-burner range and a broiler. A dated white porcelain sink was under one north window, with a modern dishwasher beside it. A long work-table, covered with a red-and-white-checked, plastic-coated tablecloth, was usually near the stove and sink. A simple dining table fit along the south wall, surrounded by a few straight-backed chairs. Dishes, glasses, and silverware were kept in various white metal cabinets. From the kitchen, there were entrances to three different rooms.

Through a swinging door to the east was a dark room lit by one small window that served as the pantry. Along each wall were rows of shelves filled with jars of canned and dried garden produce, a few commercially canned items, spices, and grains. The refrigerator was in this room; a large freezer was kept in a separate entryway. The flour mill and grains were along the north wall. Pots and pans were hung on nails against another wall. Mixing bowls, the blender, various graters, whisks, and beaters were along an adjacent wall. At times, bundles of herbs hung from the vigas. There was a near impeccable order in which everything was kept. This rather dark room seemed to exude a sort of magic from the variety of colors and shapes in all the glass jars.

The Indian Room was through a door to the west of the kitchen. The room was given this name because the house's previous Indian inhabitants, probably two centuries earlier, were said to have used its low adobe ledges for beds. The small, cool room had a brown adobe floor partially covered with a Navajo Indian rug; the adobe walls were painted white. A simple, low wooden table was the only piece of furniture. In the summer and fall, fruit was stored here. The room was used for drying fruit and herbs as well.

To the south was the dining room—a rectangular room with dark adobe floors, white walls, and a corner fireplace painted white. Double doors, with long vertical windows covered by white muslin curtains, looked out on the patio. The only furniture was a large, simple table made of sturdy, white-stained plywood—surrounded by several old wooden captain's chairs. The chairs were softened with cushions, and small Mexican weavings draped over their backs. A graceful African sculpture hung on one white wall. A small *nicho* was sculpted into the opposite wall and contained a variety of smooth river rocks and a Quan Yin statue.

The Abiquiu house provided a comfortable and productive setting for business and daily life, but Miss O'Keeffe relished her stays at Ghost Ranch in a more simple and unencumbered setting. She once remarked that she had done less to make the Ghost Ranch house hers, and that she associated a kind of freedom with it.

Cooking at the Ghost Ranch house was a somewhat different experience than at the Abiquiu home. In the Ghost Ranch kitchen, there were views of the

Kitchen Apron: O'Keeffe, Abiquiu (door from the pantry into Miss O'Keeffe's Abiquiu kitchen). © 1980 by Myron Wood.

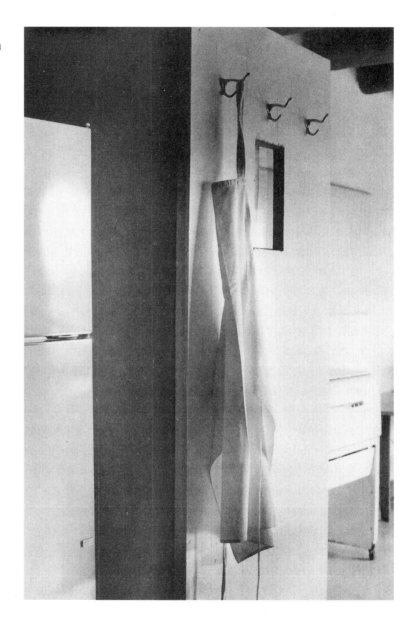

red hills and cliffs to the north, with the flagstone and sagebrush patio in another direction. The electric stove there was adequate, and the deep, old-fashioned, porcelain double sink was "a prize." The adobe walls were white, as were the wooden cupboards. The floor here was linoleum—large squares in black and white. In the corner of the kitchen, where adjacent glass windows met, there was a cozy dining area with a small, square table and built-in adobe *bancos,* or benches, for seats.

This house also had a pantry, a narrow, rectangular room with a refrigerator, a freezer, and many shelves and drawers. These shelves were filled with jars of herbs and spices, as in the Abiquiu pantry. Mixing bowls, platters, pots, and iron frying pans were packed into this little room. When Miss O'Keeffe stayed at the ranch in the summer, produce and other foods were brought daily from the Abiquiu house. Water was also brought from Abiquiu, as the ranch water was at times nearly the color of iron.

The Ghost Ranch dining room had one large window that faced the distant red cliffs. The room opened in the opposite direction onto the sagebrush-filled patio. The table was the same simple stained plywood as in Abiquiu. Built-in adobe *bancos* provided seats on two sides of the table; simple wooden chairs were the remaining seats. A corner fireplace provided warmth on cold afternoons and evenings. However, most of the meals I prepared at Ghost Ranch were served at the small kitchen table, set in its glass corner, where the Ghost Ranch cliffs and piñon trees were easily visible.

When I began working as a companion for Georgia O'Keeffe, my responsibilities included cooking many of her meals. Simple food was what she preferred, with fresh and pure ingredients. For this cookbook I have reconstructed, to the best of my recollection, many dishes that I often prepared for Miss O'Keeffe. Some recipes were developed by Miss O'Keeffe herself; all were adapted to her taste through her suggestions. Many dishes were contributions from those who worked in the O'Keeffe household. Some were influenced by Adelle Davis, Lelord Kordel, or other health food proponents of the fifties. A few are traditional foods of northern New Mexico. Within many sections, the recipes are organized according to seasonal availability of specific garden produce. These recipes are presented in the spirit of fresh flavor and good health to all who try them.

salads

Salads were a consistent part of the "noon meal" (as Miss O'Keeffe called it) and supper menus. They were valued for their fresh flavors and their wholesome, unspoiled nutrients.

A few varieties of lettuce were grown in the garden, generally supplying the household from late May until September. Miss O'Keeffe insisted that these greens be picked carefully, then washed and patted dry so that the dressing would adhere thoroughly to the lettuce. The herbs, too, were snipped with care, then prepared similarly.

Miss O'Keeffe preferred a substantial amount of a variety of herbs in the salad dressing, as she savored their fresh taste. The herb patch in the garden, although rather small and somewhat overgrown, was quite hardy. Miss O'Keeffe acquainted me with wiry tarragon, feathery dill, stalky lovage, bushy green and purple basil, and other herbs. A number of recipes included herbs, as Miss O'Keeffe was fond of their flavors and considered them to have many beneficial properties.

Classic Summer Salad

Two or three varieties of lettuce (bibb, butter, red-leaf, green-leaf)
Several leaves of sorrel (optional)
Herb Salad Dressing

Wash, then pat or spin dry, two or three varieties of lettuce and the sorrel, enough for the preferred number of servings. Tear the lettuce and sorrel by hand into manageable bite-sized pieces. Add the following Herb Salad Dressing.

Herb Salad Dressing

Wash the herbs and pat them dry. Then chop all herbs medium fine, except the chives. Blend the olive and safflower oils with a fork, add the lemon juice and mustard. Squeeze one medium garlic clove through a garlic press and add it to the liquid. Then add the chopped herbs to the dressing. Add herb salt and freshly ground pepper to taste. Add a pinch of sugar if the mixture is too sour. Allow this dressing to stand for an hour, if possible, so that the herb and garlic flavors can permeate the dressing. This quantity will dress a salad for 4–6 people.

Before serving the salad, rub a wooden salad bowl with a garlic clove split in half. Add the lettuce to the bowl. Pour the dressing over the lettuce and toss the salad. Chop the chives into ¼-inch pieces and sprinkle them on top.

Note: There are quite a number of herbs included in this dressing. For practicality, use the herbs available or preferred. Sliced or quartered sweet cherry tomatoes, thinly sliced small radishes, or chopped and seeded cucumbers are possible additions to this salad. In the salad dressing, a variation for the lemon juice is balsamic vinegar; the vinegar lends a rich, slightly sweet taste to the dressing.

2 teaspoons herbs: lovage, tarragon, dill, basil, parsley
2 tablespoons olive oil
2 tablespoons safflower oil, or other high-quality vegetable oil
1 teaspoon lemon juice, or more to taste
¼ teaspoon whole seed mustard
2 garlic cloves
Herb salt, to taste
Freshly ground pepper, to taste
Pinch of sugar (optional)
Chives, as garnish

Watercress Salad

There are many springs in Abiquiu and in the nearby village of Barranco, where I lived. At times, watercress was available along the springs on Miss O'Keeffe's land. But most of the year I could pick watercress along the Barranco *acequia,* which channeled several springs as they seeped out of the hills. The springs were a constant temperature, so the watercress grew year-round. At times, the watercress was so thick that only a narrow stream of water could be seen winding through. Watercress salad was almost constantly available. These fresh greens provide a good source of vitamins A and C, potassium, and calcium.

2 substantial bunches watercress (about 2 ounces)
Herb Salad Dressing
½ garlic clove

Pick or buy at least 2 substantial bunches of watercress with delicate stems. Wash the watercress carefully, especially if it is hand-picked. Separate the tough stem bottoms from the remainder of the plant. (If the plant is blooming, the flowers are edible as well.) Spin or pat the leaves dry. Put the watercress in a wooden salad bowl that has been rubbed with half a garlic clove. Add Herb Salad Dressing (p. 3). Serves 4–6.

Note: If the watercress taste is too strong and spicy, add some lettuce to the salad. This will balance the watercress flavor. Sliced sweet radishes, tomatoes, jicama, or oranges are a nice addition to this salad.

I do not know the origin of this recipe; however, it could be related to one of the cookbooks stuffed into the Abiquiu kitchen bookshelf. I remember *The Fanny Farmer Boston Cooking School Cookbook, The Joy of Cooking, Let's Eat Right to Stay Fit, Let's Cook It Right, Cook Right, Live Longer,* and several others. But perhaps the most valuable book was a red loose-leaf notebook containing Miss O'Keeffe's favorite recipes. This was affectionately referred to as "Mary's Book," named after a previous staff member who had compiled it. That notebook was continually consulted and revised to include new recipes or to improve on older ones.

When her eyes had been stronger, Miss O'Keeffe had the habit of reading cookbooks before she went to bed. She remarked that they were enjoyable nighttime company, providing brief and pleasant reading.

In her nineties, she still enjoyed listening to recipes and adjusting them to her own taste. As she had collected a number of healthy and flavorful recipes, she would occasionally laugh and comment, "We should write a cookbook."

Beet and Green Bean Salad

Cut the beets into halves or quarters. Then cook them in boiling water until they are tender. Let the beets cool slightly, then peel them. Cut them into bite-size pieces about ⅜-inch thick. Snap or cut the ends off the green beans, then snap or cut them into 1-inch pieces. Remove any tough, fibrous "strings." Boil the beans for 6–8 minutes, or until tender, then drain and put in a bowl.

While the vegetables are still slightly warm, add the Herb Salad Dressing (p. 3). Let the salad stand at room temperature or chill it for at least 1 hour.

Note: This is a very refreshing mid-summer salad. It is also very pretty as the beets will tint the salad. This salad is good to prepare ahead of time; make extra as it keeps well. It can be served in a menu of Baked Chicken with Lemon (p. 58), baked potatoes, and Vanilla Ice Cream (p. 92) with fresh raspberries.

5–6 medium-sized beets
¾ pound green beans, or combination of green, purple, and yellow beans
Herb Salad Dressing

Tomato Aspic

During all seasons, Miss O'Keeffe customarily walked in the morning, then again in the late afternoon before supper. At Ghost Ranch she walked along the path to the cliffs or beside the dirt road by the red clay hills. In Abiquiu, her walk took her round the wide driveway with its grand view of the Chama River Valley. Following each turn around the driveway, she would place a smooth river rock on the stucco windowsill—often gathering a collection of seven to ten stones.

When she walked, Miss O'Keeffe often wore a black felt, Western-style hat with a string that fit under her chin. "When I first got it, it was so terribly new-looking that I carried rocks around in it—that put holes in it right away," she recalled.

2 cups fresh tomato sauce, or high-quality canned sauce
1 envelope unflavored gelatin
2 tablespoons lemon juice
Dash of Worcestershire sauce
Fresh chives, as garnish
Fresh horseradish (optional)
Lettuce or watercress salad, as accompaniment

In a small saucepan, heat ½ cup of the tomato sauce with the gelatin. When the gelatin is dissolved, add the remaining ingredients. Then pour the mixture into molds, or a muffin tin, and chill until firm.

Turn the molds upside down and slowly pour warm water over each portion you wish to serve. Hold a plate underneath as the aspic loosens from each mold. Serve the aspic on top of 2 or 3 small lettuce leaves, fresh watercress, or surround it with Classic Summer Salad (p. 2) or Watercress Salad (p. 4). Chop fresh chives in ¼-inch pieces to garnish the aspic. Freshly grated horseradish is also quite good with this.

Note: Home-canned tomato sauce was preferred in any recipe calling for this ingredient; however, commercially canned sauce was used if that was the only type available. There were very few commercially canned goods in the O'Keeffe household pantry.

Miss O'Keeffe's favorite foods were often simple, almost austere, like many of the forms she painted. She once advised me about designs for my weavings. She admired the lines in Japanese and Chinese calligraphy and referred to them when she told me to create "lines that speak" in my designs. Also, she said to think of design in relation to spatial variety "like your hand—big spaces, smaller ones, and a place to rest." I was to draw the designs quite large and to make several of them so that I could choose which was best. She thought that I should make a white weaving with a big blue circle. A few years later, she made a simple design that I translated into a weaving for one of her friends.

Orange Gelatin

Measure ½ cup of orange juice into a small saucepan. Add the gelatin, then slowly heat the mixture until the gelatin dissolves. Stir in the remaining juice and add sugar to taste if the orange juice is tart. Pour the orange juice mixture into any preferred mold(s). Chill until firm. Loosen from the mold with warm water. The orange gelatin can be served on small lettuce leaves, garnished with watercress, fresh mint, or chives.

2 cups fresh-squeezed
   orange juice
1 envelope unflavored
   gelatin
Sugar (optional)
Lettuce, watercress, mint,
   or chives, as garnish

Guacamole

We usually ate this as a salad on fresh, small lettuce leaves. The best avocadoes were contributed by Miss O'Keeffe's youngest sister, Claudia, who brought them from her yard in Beverly Hills (or "Beverly" as Claudia called it). Claudia often stayed in Abiquiu for a few months in the summer to supervise the garden while her sister stayed at Ghost Ranch. She brought one staff person with her and a miniature Yorkshire terrier. Claudia wore a wide-brimmed straw hat as she carefully walked the garden paths, tending areas here and there or picking produce that was ready for the table.

2 ripe, creamy avocadoes
1 small tomato
2 teaspoons finely diced white onion
1 medium garlic clove
2 teaspoons lemon juice
Herb salt to taste
Lettuce, as accompaniment
Paprika, as garnish

Scoop the avocado fruit out of the peel and into a bowl. Discard the pit. Mash the avocadoes with a fork until they have a rather creamy consistency. Finely chop the tomato (discarding excess juice), then add it to the mashed avocado; also add the onion. Squeeze the garlic through a press and add it to the mixture. Stir the lemon juice into the guacamole and add herb salt to taste. Serve on small lettuce leaves. Garnish with paprika. Serves 4.

Miss O'Keeffe frequently bought her eggs from an elderly woman who raised chickens near the El Rito road. The two women had known each other for many years. When the O'Keeffe household was out of eggs, the painter would call her neighbor and ask for eggs in simple, careful Spanish. When we went to pick them up, the woman meticulously washed each one and gently placed it in a container, while telling the most recent story about her family, or her chickens and her dogs, in a colorful mixture of Spanish and English.

Herb-Stuffed Eggs

Boil the eggs for 12–15 minutes. Place them in cold water to cool for about 10 minutes, then carefully peel off the shells. Slice each egg in half. Remove the solid yolks and place them in a mixing bowl. Then mix in the mustard and yogurt. Mash these ingredients with a fork until the mixture is creamy and without lumps. Add herb salt to taste.

Select any number of herbs desired. Chop the herbs finely, keeping each one separate. For every egg (2 halves), separate about 1 tablespoon of yolk mixture into a smaller bowl. Mix in at least ¼–½ teaspoon of the desired herb per egg. When using dried herbs, curry, or other spices, use smaller amounts (⅛ teaspoon or less). Fill each egg half with a slightly heaping herb/spice-and-egg yolk mixture. Repeat this process with the next herb or spice of your choice. This recipe is best when prepared to individual tastes. Feel free to experiment with a variety and quantity of herbs and spices. These eggs are rather unusual as they contain a surprising array of flavors.

6 fresh eggs
1 teaspoon mustard
3 tablespoons yogurt
Herb salt, to taste
Several leaves of
    tarragon, basil, sage,
    dill, chives, marjoram,
    lovage, or any other
    preferred herbs
Curry powder, or any
    other preferred spices

Cottage Cheese and Orange Salad

During my initial interview with Miss O'Keeffe, one of her first questions was "Can you cook?" I knew how to cook for my own taste and gradually learned her preferences. If a meal had been particularly well prepared, Miss O'Keeffe might say it was "scandalously good."

This is one of the first salads Miss O'Keeffe taught me how to make. As simple as it is, she gave exact instructions as to how I should make it. This salad was served in a shallow white bowl. All meals were served on plain white china. Salt cellars were small, white, porcelain, footed sake cups with tiny shell spoons. The silverware was a simple style in stainless steel. Napkins were fringed white cotton. They were made soft by many washings and were kept perfectly white with continuous care. Straw mats in natural or bright colors completed the usual table setting.

---

1 orange
¼ small onion
½ cup cottage cheese
    per person
Chives, as garnish

Peel the orange so that only the thin membrane is visible (no pith). Separate the orange into halves and cut it into ¼-inch slices, removing all seeds. Then separate the slices into the individual sections. Slice the onion into very thin slivers, then chop them into ½-inch pieces.

Scoop the cottage cheese into small bowls. Arrange 10–12 orange sections on top of each serving, then sprinkle 2 teaspoons of onion slivers on top. Garnish with chives cut ¼-inch long.

This salad was sometimes served with the noon meal in the late summer and fall. Miss O'Keeffe and her business manager, Juan Hamilton, would often eat lunch together. Miss O'Keeffe and Hamilton had great respect for each other. One day after a magazine interview with the two of them, Miss O'Keeffe commented, "They won't find people like Juan and me very often. I'm sure we gave that girl really something special."

Beet and Onion Salad

Cut off the roots and save the beet greens for another meal. Wash the beets well. Boil them for 20–30 minutes, or until they are tender. Cool them slightly and peel with a knife. (The skins slide off most easily when the beets are still rather hot.) Slice the beets into rounds no more than ⅛-inch thick. Peel the onion and slice it into rounds no more than ⅛-inch thick. Put the vegetables into a shallow bowl.

Mix the white wine vinegar with the sugar; stir until the sugar is dissolved. Pour this liquid over the beets and onions and gently stir to combine ingredients. Let the salad stand a few hours so that the dressing can permeate the vegetables. This salad can be garnished with fresh chives or parsley. Serves 4.

4 small beets
1 small sweet white onion
2 tablespoons white wine vinegar
¼ teaspoon sugar
Chives or parsley, as garnish

Cabbage Salad with Apple and Walnuts

This is a fall or winter salad, a good accompaniment for a light supper, with either an oil-and-vinegar or a yogurt dressing. During supper by the fire, Miss O'Keeffe often talked about the years when she lived in New York (1918 to 1946) with her husband Alfred Stieglitz, the well-known photographer and proponent of modern art through his gallery "291." (Miss O'Keeffe first came to New Mexico in the summer of 1929. After that time, she spent summers in New Mexico and winters in New York with Stieglitz.)

She described the people she knew at that time: "There was a small group of people in literature, art, and music who cared about the *best* of all those things. Now, money has taken over. People are involved or contribute because it's good table talk, social status. I remember when almost everyone was too poor to buy a picture," she said. "I'm glad I lived part of my life in the city," she said. "I knew all that was happening in the art world for quite awhile." When asked if she missed the city now, she replied, "It's for the birds."

½ small green or
    red cabbage
1 small apple with a sweet
    and tart flavor
½ cup walnuts
Herb Salad Dressing

Cut the cabbage half into 2 pieces and core them. Then slice the cabbage into fine shreds no wider than ⅛-inch and into segments 2 inches long. Core and quarter the apple, then cut it into small chunks about ¼-inch thick and ½-inch square. (You may want to peel a commercially produced, nonorganic apple.) Chop or break the walnuts so that they are about the same size as the apple chunks.

Mix the cabbage, apple, and walnuts together in a salad bowl. Add the Herb Salad Dressing (p. 3) and stir again. Serves 4–6.

Classic Summer Salad with Herb Salad Dressing, p. 2 and 3

Minestrone Soup, p. 21

Fresh Vegetables

Beef Stew, p. 61

Green Chile Chicken Enchiladas, p.70

Posole, p. 74

Granola, p. 88

Biscochitos, p. 99

soups

"**Soup** is such a comfort," Miss O'Keeffe would sometimes say. Soups were generally the focus of the supper menu, often served with a salad, a vegetable, bread or crackers, and a dessert.

Before supper in the summer, we would often take a walk toward the red cliffs at Ghost Ranch. Miss O'Keeffe's two dogs, chows named Inca and Jingo, would accompany us as we walked in the overgrown ruts of an old dirt road. Inca was a black male, and Jingo was a red-blond female. Miss O'Keeffe referred to these two as "the people" and was quite fond of them. She had owned chows before and found them to be good companions. During our walks, these dogs usually stayed rather close to their owner, unless they spotted a jackrabbit. Then they would dash over the red and gray clay hills, yelping with excitement. If it was hot, we would all pause in the shade of a particularly bushy piñon tree, then anticipate our return to the cool ranch kitchen for supper.

Buttermilk Soup

2 cups buttermilk
2 egg yolks
1 scant tablespoon sugar
1 teaspoon lemon rind,
   finely grated

Measure the buttermilk into a mixing bowl. Separate the egg yolks from the whites and combine the yolks and sugar with the buttermilk using a rotary beater. Grate 1 teaspoon of zest (the outer yellow rind without any white pith) from a fresh lemon. Add it to the buttermilk. Beat all ingredients until well blended. Pour into individual bowls. A pinch of grated rind can be reserved to garnish the soup. (You may want to scrub commercially produced lemons before grating to clean off wax and pesticide residue.)

On a hot summer day, this is a very pleasing soup. It can be prepared in advance, then chilled in the mixing bowl before serving. Beat the soup again before pouring it into individual bowls. This soup can be served with steamed Spinach (p. 35), Classic Summer Salad (p. 2), rice crackers and cream cheese with herbs, and fresh fruit. Serves 2–3.

This is a lovely late spring soup. At this time of year, there would often be a bouquet of irises or lilacs on the table, in a simple clear glass vase. Miss O'Keeffe began talking one afternoon about her limited eyesight and the flowers. "You know, the way I see this flower is really quite beautiful—the outside petals I can see, an' the inside is very soft, barely there. You couldn't see it the way I do." She had formerly had very good eyesight, both far and near. She was annoyed by this change, but she seldom complained.

Fresh Pea Soup

Cook the fresh peas in a small amount of boiling water for 5–8 minutes, or until tender. Then drain them. Liquefy the peas, chicken broth, onion, and mint together in the blender on a high setting until they are a creamy consistency. Slowly heat the soup, but do not simmer it. Garnish with a pinch of finely chopped chives. Serves 3–4.

2 cups fresh peas
2 cups homemade chicken broth, or high-quality canned broth
1 tablespoon chopped onion
1 tablespoon mint
Herb salt, to taste
Chives, as garnish

Quelite Soup

Quelites, also known as lamb's quarters, are edible weeds that are related to spinach. These greens have a high content of vitamins C and A, and calcium. They grow in gardens, fields, and along the roadsides in northern New Mexico and across the United States. In the springtime, this plant is collected and eaten raw in salads or cooked as a vegetable. Surplus quelites were frozen after they were cleaned, for a winter supply.

Although this soup has simple ingredients, it is rather difficult to balance the flavor correctly. If the soup did not taste quite right, Miss O'Keeffe would say that it had not been "made with love."

Approximately 3 cups cleaned, tightly packed fresh quelite leaves, or 1½ cups thawed, frozen leaves
1 tablespoon chopped onion
1 tablespoon butter
2 cups milk, or home-made chicken broth
1 tablespoon Soup Mix, p. 19 (optional)
Herb salt, to taste

Steam the fresh quelite leaves for 3–4 minutes. Sauté the onion in the butter until it is transparent. Then put the quelites and onions in a blender. Add the milk or broth, Soup Mix, if desired, and herb salt to taste. Blend at high speed until finely liquefied. The liquid should be the consistency of light cream. Heat the soup slowly and serve it immediately. Do not simmer. Serves 2–3.

This is a delicious, mild, summer soup. The Soup Mix recipe below is a mixture of brewer's yeast, soy flour, powdered milk, and powdered kelp, inspired by Lelord Kordel. This mixture boosts the nutritional value of any food in which it is used. Miss O'Keeffe requested that it be added to many soups and breads. A jar of this mixture was always kept available. It does have a strong taste, which can interfere with mild soups such as this. Use of this soup powder is optional and quantity is up to individual taste.

Lelord Kordel wrote many books on health and preventive medicine. He stressed the importance of sensible eating and the elimination of processed foods and synthetic drugs. He promoted a return to natural foods and remedies.

Cucumber Soup

Wash and peel the cucumbers. Split them in half and scoop the seeds out with a spoon. Chop the cucumbers roughly and put them in a blender or food processor. Add the milk, onion, parsley, Soup mix, and herb salt to the blender. Blend at a high setting until the ingredients are well mixed. Serve cold, garnished with parsley sprigs. Serves 3.

2 medium cucumbers
2 cups milk
1 tablespoon minced onion
1 tablespoon chopped parsley
2 teaspoons Soup Mix
Herb salt, to taste

Soup Mix

Measure these ingredients into a glass storage container. Cover with a tight-fitting lid and shake the jar to combine the ingredients thoroughly. Add this to creamed soups and breads to taste.

1½ cups powdered milk
1 cup soy flour
½ cup kelp
1 cup brewer's yeast

Tomato Soup with Lovage

Lovage was Miss O'Keeffe's favorite herb. The plant is a tall, hardy perennial that is easy to grow in most areas of the United States. The leaves look somewhat like celery, but have a stronger taste. Lovage adds delightful flavor to salads, soups, and meat dishes.

Lovage is not a well-known herb in the Southwest. It is native to the Mediterranean area and was used by the Greeks and Romans as a medicine. In Europe during the Middle Ages, it was used as a treatment for a variety of illnesses. Some European women developed the custom of wearing lovage around their necks when meeting their lovers, and lovage was often added to love potions. More recently, lovage has been used to treat stomach disorders, jaundice, and urinary problems.

From the mid- to late summer, this herb was gathered, tied together in bunches, and hung from the vigas to dry for winter use. Several large jars of dried lovage added to the array of dried herbs on the pantry shelves.

---

2 cups fresh tomato sauce, from 3 pounds tomatoes, or 1 can tomato soup
2 teaspoons butter
2 teaspoons unbleached flour
1 cup water, milk, or cream
Sugar, to taste
Herb salt, to taste
2 or 3 sprigs of lovage with a few leaves on each sprig

Scald the tomatoes for 1 minute in boiling water, then remove the skins. Cut the tomatoes in quarters and remove the stems, cores, and seeds. Simmer on low heat in a saucepan until the tomatoes are soft. Then push them through a fine sieve or food mill. Set the resulting sauce aside.

Melt the butter in the saucepan. Add the flour and stir to combine into a roux. When the flour and butter are sizzling, add the tomato sauce slowly and stir continuously to keep the mixture smooth. Add water, milk, or cream until the purée is the consistency of heavy cream. The addition of a little sugar will cut down on the acidity of the tomatoes. Then add herb salt to taste. (If commercially canned soup is used, prepare the soup according to directions on the can, using either water or milk.)

Add the lovage sprigs. Heat the soup slowly. The lovage will impart its flavor to the soup and transform it into something "quite special" as Miss O'Keeffe would say. Serve the soup with a lovage sprig in each bowl. The leaves can be eaten, but they are rather strong. This serves 2 or 3. Lovage is also used in Herb Salad Dressing (p. 3), Herb-Stuffed Eggs (p. 9), Chicken Soup (p. 31), Beef Stew (p. 61), and Meatloaf (p. 62).

This was the perfect soup to highlight the flavors of the garden in early August, when all the vegetables were available. If the Abiquiu house was still warm from the heat of the day, we might eat supper in the Roofless Room. This room was spanned by six or seven vigas at varying distances and widely spaced *latillas* (smaller round beams) with wire screen sandwiched between. The sky was visible between the spaces in the beams, creating the feeling of being out-of-doors. One west window looked out to the garden; a ceramic bull "guarded" that window. Three black cooking grates decorated the white stucco walls. The table was a thin sandstone slab supported by large bricks on a gravel "floor." At midday, shadows from the beams contributed an array of abstract patterns on the white walls.

In a large soup pot, sauté the onion and celery in the oil. When they become tender and transparent, add the chicken broth and bring the mixture to a low simmer. Squeeze the garlic through a press and stir it into the liquid. Add all remaining vegetables, except the spinach, and simmer for 2 hours. Stir in the spinach during the last 2 minutes of cooking. Add the herb salt and freshly ground pepper to taste. Serves 4–6.

Cooked navy beans, kidney beans, fava beans, or garbanzo beans are also good in this soup. A small amount of pre-cooked pasta is another addition. Finely chopped parsley and freshly grated Parmesan or Romano cheese can be added before serving.

Minestrone Soup

2 tablespoons safflower oil, or olive oil
An assortment of vegetables, which could include:
  ½ cup minced onion
  ⅓ cup diced celery
  1 cup diced carrots
  1 cup shredded cabage
  1 cup string beans, cut into ½-inch pieces
  1 cup diced zucchini
  2 medium tomatoes, peeled, seeded, and chopped roughly
  1 cup chopped spinach
4 cups chicken or vegetable broth
1 or 2 garlic cloves
Herb salt, to taste
Freshly ground pepper, to taste
Cooked navy beans, kidney beans, fava beans, or garbanzo beans (optional)
Precooked pasta (optional)
Parmesan or Romano cheese, as garnish
Parsley, as garnish

Leek and Potato Soup

After a pleasant supper of soup and salads or vegetables, we would often listen to music on the high-quality stereo system in the "sitting room" or studio. Miss O'Keeffe had wide-ranging musical taste. She enjoyed Gregorian chants and the early music of Monteverdi and Gesualdo. She collected music of Bach, Beethoven, and Schubert, as well as Aaron Copland and Edgar Varese. She spoke fondly of the winter when she and a friend had listened to all the Beethoven sonatas. Wanda Landowska and Arthur Schnabel were two performers she enjoyed. She also admired Bach's cello suites performed by Pablo Casals.

4 large leeks
2 stalks celery
4 tablespoons butter
5–6 potatoes with a fine consistency
2–3 cups cream, or a mixture of milk and cream
Herb salt, to taste
Freshly ground pepper
1–2 tablespoons butter for added richness (optional)
Parsley, as garnish

Clean the leeks and chop them roughly. Peel off any tough strands from the celery and chop it as well. Sauté the leeks and celery in the butter in a 2-quart saucepan. When they are tender, remove the pan from the heat.

Clean and peel the potatoes and cut them into chunks. Put them in the saucepan with the leeks and celery. Cover the vegetables with water, bring to a boil, and cook until tender. Transfer to a fine sieve and, using a pestle, push the potatoes, leeks, celery, and cooking water through the mesh into a large mixing bowl. Then transfer the thick purée back to the saucepan. Add cream until the liquid is the consistency of heavy cream. Sprinkle in herb salt and freshly ground pepper to taste. One or 2 tablespoons of butter can be added for extra richness. Garnish with finely chopped parsley. Serves 6–8.

Corn soup, using frozen garden corn, is very pleasant-tasting, especially in the winter. During a winter supper, we would sit in the peaceful, white dining room by a cheerful fire. In this room there was very little formal art. An African mask—a woman's long, dignified face carved in dark wood—hung on one wall. "That head," Miss O'Keeffe said, "was something left from the first show of Negro art in the country. If I did a painting and placed it next to the mask—and the painting looked pretty good beside it—I knew the painting was good. But if it couldn't stand up to it, the painting could be better."

Corn Soup

Put the fresh, raw corn in a blender container. Add the 2 cups of milk, minced onion, Soup Mix (p. 19), and herb salt. Blend at the highest setting for about 15 seconds. Use a pestle to push the liquid through a fine sieve into a pan. Heat the soup slowly, stirring it continuously as it thickens. Serve immediately. Do not simmer. Garnish with finely chopped chives or parsley. Serves 3.

2 cups corn scraped from fresh-picked or frozen ears
2 cups milk
1 tablespoon minced onion
1 tablespoon Soup Mix (optional)
Herb salt, to taste
Chives or parsley, as garnish

Beet Soup

During June through September, when the garden was most productive, Miss O'Keeffe would often walk with me to pick the vegetables she wanted for supper. She would consider what was ripe and what flavors would be pleasing, then supper would be served near six o'clock. Meals were generally prepared according to the following preferred schedule: breakfast at 7 a.m., the noon meal at 12 o'clock, and supper at 6 p.m. This schedule is one example of the patterns that suited the artist in her nineties.

4 medium-sized beets without tops or roots
3 cups mild homemade beef or chicken broth, or high-quality canned broth
1 tablespoon lemon juice
1 tablespoon chopped onion
Herb salt, to taste
Sugar (optional)
Plain yogurt, as garnish (1 tablespoon per serving)

Boil the beets until tender. Cool them to room temperature and peel. Chop the beets roughly and place them in a blender with the broth, lemon juice, and onion. Blend on a high setting until well puréed. Add herb salt to taste and a pinch of sugar, if desired. This soup can be served cold or hot. Top with a dollop of yogurt in each bowl before serving. Serves 4.

This is a very tasty and elegant soup. As we ate our soup, we would talk of the day's events. One particular evening I told how I had climbed Pedernal, the flat-topped volcanic mountain depicted in several of Miss O'Keeffe's paintings. She began to speak of her attitude toward aging: "I've done all right on my other paths of life, but this last one—this ancient one—it's harder to find things to do as good as being on top of a mountain. I *like* to think of someone tearing around in the mountains."

Mushroom Soup

Clean the mushrooms if necessary, then chop them roughly. In a saucepan, sauté the onion in the butter until the onion is transparent. Then pour the chicken broth into the saucepan and bring the mixture to a low simmer for about 3 minutes. Next, put the mushrooms in a blender, add the chicken broth, and blend to a very smooth consistency on a high setting.

Pour the blended mixture back into the saucepan and add the cream. Heat the soup slowly until very hot, but do not simmer. Add herb salt to taste.

Pour 1 tablespoon of dry sherry into each warmed serving bowl. Ladle the soup into each bowl and stir gently to mix the sherry and soup. Grate a pinch of fresh nutmeg over each serving. Serves 4–6.

This is a very elegant and rich soup which is well complemented with French bread, Watercress Salad (p. 4), and Apple Pie (p. 96).

¾ pound fresh mushrooms
2 tablespoons butter
3 tablespoons onion, roughly chopped
2 cups homemade chicken broth, or high-quality canned broth
2 cups light cream
Herb salt, to taste
Dry sherry, as directed
Nutmeg, as garnish

Watercress Soup

The availability of watercress practically year-round made this soup one we could enjoy throughout the winter. We would sit by the dining room fire on a cold, dark evening and take great pleasure in this lovely soup.

Miss O'Keeffe had several fireplaces in the Abiquiu house. The caretaker built all the fires with individual care. He would chop different sizes of kindling so that the wood was arranged in three or more graduated vertical layers. The fires were quite easy to light, as the shorter, finer kindling was toward the front. Miss O'Keeffe would remark admiringly that none of his fires ever looked the same. Framed by the arched white mouth of the fireplace, the light-colored kindling against the deep, black-crusted adobe presented a soft abstract pattern.

1 substantial bunch of watercress (approximately 2 cups, when chopped)
2 cups homemade chicken broth, or high-quality canned broth
2 eggs at room temperature
Herb salt to taste, if using homemade chicken broth

Clean and chop the watercress into 1-inch lengths, discarding tough lower stems. Heat the chicken broth in a medium-sized saucepan. Break the eggs into a separate bowl and lightly beat with a fork to thoroughly mix them. When the broth simmers, add the watercress. Then lower the heat and slowly add the eggs to the soup in a thin stream, so that the eggs cook quickly in delicate threads. Remove the soup from the heat and serve. Serves 2–3.

Often at supper, Miss O'Keeffe would reminisce about Alfred Stieglitz and his Gallery 291. One evening, speaking to a New York art dealer, she recalled "My husband said that I had a knack for making rich friends who didn't like pictures." However, Stieglitz was apparently very careful about those to whom he did sell her paintings, as if very few people "deserved" to own one. From time to time, Miss O'Keeffe had to coax him to sell more work so that she would be able to make a living that year.

Pumpkin Soup

Try to use fresh, baked pumpkin with a naturally sweet taste. Mash the pumpkin, then put it in the blender with the chicken broth, cream or half and half. Blend this at a high setting until smooth, then pour into a heavy, medium-sized saucepan. Slowly heat but do not simmer. Season with herb salt and nutmeg. Add more nutmeg as a garnish if desired. Serves 4–6.

1 cup baked fresh pumpkin (or Acorn or Turban squash)
3 cups chicken broth
1 cup half and half or cream
½ teaspoon freshly ground nutmeg
¼ teaspoon herb salt

Almond Soup

At times, Miss O'Keeffe spoke of winter memories from Wisconsin when she was young. Going to the horse barn to ask the man to saddle the horses for pulling the sled, snow crunching under her feet, sleigh and toboggan rides in the moonlight, making an imprint of her coat in the snow, square dancing and her father fiddling.

On cold nights, by fire and candlelight, this almond soup was quite delicate but substantial.

½ cup chopped onions
½ cup whole, blanched
   almonds
2 tablespoons safflower
   oil
1 cup chicken broth
1 cup milk
½ teaspoon herb salt, or
   to taste
Parsley, as garnish
Freshly ground pepper

Using a heavy skillet, slowly sauté the onions and almonds in the oil until golden. Puree the onions and almonds, the chicken broth and milk in the blender at a high setting until the almonds are finely grained. Heat and add herb salt to taste. Do not simmer this soup. Garnish with finely chopped parsley and a little freshly ground pepper. Serves 4–6.

Georgia O'Keeffe had long been friends with the photographer Laura Gilpin. They spoke about their respective art endeavors by phone one afternoon. Miss O'Keeffe described her current approach to painting, influenced by her poor eyesight: "I can't really see very well; but if you know what you're doing, you don't have to see."

Avocado Soup

Scoop the avocado fruit out of the peel and discard the pit. Put the avocado, milk, and curry powder into the blender. Blend on high setting until totally smooth. Heat on low setting until hot; do not allow soup to simmer. Serve with a pinch of curry powder sprinkled on top, or with very finely chopped chives or parsley. A small amount of white pepper is an optional addition.

1 medium ripe avocado
2 cups milk
1 teaspoon curry powder
¼ teaspoon herb salt
Chives, or parsley, as
    garnish
White pepper (optional)

Steamed Chicken Soup

This soup is Chinese in origin. Miss O'Keeffe appreciated Chinese art, philosophy, poetry, and food. She spoke admiringly of Chinese watercolors and calligraphy. The only poetry she really enjoyed was Chinese, particularly a collection called *The Jade Mountain,* translated by her late friend Witter Bynner, who had lived in Santa Fe in the 1950s. The *Tao Te Ching* was another selection we read. One February evening, we began *Journey to the West: The Monkey King,* translated by Anthony C. Yu. The book was so enchanting that we read it both evenings and mornings, beside many a fire.

2 cups homemade chicken broth, or high-quality canned broth

2 eggs at room temperature

Herb salt to taste, if using homemade chicken broth (see Watercress Soup, p. 26)

Coriander, as garnish

Prepare a steamer that can accommodate 2 or 3 soup bowls (the Chinese bamboo steamers are excellent for this purpose). The water in the steamer should be brought to a simmer. In a small mixing bowl, gently but thoroughly combine the eggs with the chicken broth using a rotary beater or whisk. Pour this mixture into 2 or 3 soup bowls. Place the soup bowls in the steamer. Steam the soup for 5–7 minutes, or until the egg and broth are a delicate custard consistency. Garnish with finely chopped coriander leaves. Serves 2–3.

During the 1960s and 1970s, many prominent magazines featured interviews with Georgia O'Keeffe, along with photographs of both her houses. During supper one evening she recalled the occasion when a female staff member from *House Beautiful* had come to the Abiquiu house and was straightening everything ני so meticulously that it no longer looked like the painter's house. At one point, when the woman was making every curtain pleat perfect, Miss O'Keeffe could not resist saying to her, "You know, you'd make a first-class maid."

Chicken Soup

Measure the chicken broth into a 2-quart pan. Add the vegetables and the garlic squeezed through a press and simmer them for 15 minutes. In a small pan, melt the butter over very low heat, then add the flour, and cook the roux until it is gently bubbling. Separate ½ cup of broth from the large pan and use a wire whisk to add this to the roux. When the roux and the broth are thoroughly blended and smooth, use the whisk to incorporate this mixture into the liquid simmering in the larger pan. Add the cooked chicken and herbs. Season with herb salt and pepper to taste. Simmer until the vegetables are tender. Serves 4.

4 cups homemade
    chicken broth
1 cup diced carrots
½ small onion, minced
2 garlic cloves
1 tablespoon butter or oil
2 teaspoons unbleached
    flour
1½ cups boned, cooked
    chicken
½ teaspoon chopped
    fresh summer savory
1 teaspoon chopped
    fresh lovage
Herb salt, to taste
Pepper, to taste

vegetables

Because the garden produced vegetables from June to September, it was not uncommon to have spinach, tomatoes, or green chiles with breakfast, or to include four or five vegetables in both the noon meal and supper.

Steam cooking was the primary method used for preparing many vegetables. In the O'Keeffe household, there was a large, round stainless steel steamer with three sections: a shallow base for water, a steaming "platter" with several holes, and a lid about 5 inches tall. Vegetables, small bowls of soup, and other foods could be cooked in this large steamer. For smaller amounts of vegetables, a collapsible stainless steel steamer was used. Miss O'Keeffe and I timed steaming rates for each vegetable so that flavor and texture were retained.

Steamed vegetables were often served with a touch of a butter-and-oil mixture and herb salt. The butter mixture was made by hand mixing ½ cup of softened butter and ½ cup of safflower oil in a small mixing bowl, then spooning the mixture into smaller round containers for table use. This mixture tastes like butter, but does not contain as much cholesterol as pure butter. Other low cholesterol oils, such as peanut, sunflower, or canola oils, can also be used.

Wild asparagus grows in several treasured spots beside irrigation ditches in northern New Mexico villages. It can be picked in early June. Local friends would sometimes bring Miss O'Keeffe a gift of wild asparagus, knowing how much she enjoyed this vegetable.

Wild Asparagus

1 bunch of wild (or cultivated) asparagus
(about 12 ounces)
Butter/oil, to taste, or for
sautéeing
Herb salt, to taste
Freshly ground pepper

Wash the asparagus carefully to remove all fine sand. Cut the woody part of the stems off, keeping the asparagus in long pieces. This tender, young asparagus can be steamed or sautéed.

To steam, place the asparagus inside a steamer and cook for 5–7 minutes (until the stems are somewhat tender when pricked with a fork). Serve with a bit of butter/oil, herb salt to taste, and freshly ground pepper.

To sauté, melt one tablespoon of butter/oil in a frying pan. When the butter bubbles, add the asparagus and sauté for 5 minutes on medium-low heat. Sprinkle herb salt over aspara-gus to taste. Serves 2–3.

"Wash the spinach with the leaves down, stems up," Miss O'Keeffe would say. She had many precise guidelines for food preparation. When mixing ingredients, she explained, "Dig down and lift." To scrape out a pan, she instructed, "Scrape with the edge of the spoon, not the tip." She had an ability to describe precisely the manner in which her food should be prepared, as well as the taste and texture that she desired.

Spinach

Select at least 1 pound of spinach for 2 people. Wash the spinach 2 or 3 times to make sure all the fine sand or dirt is washed away. When the steamer is simmering, add the spinach to the basket and cover. Steam for 3–4 minutes, depending on the tenderness desired. Place each serving on a warmed plate. If desired, slice through the spinach a few times to divide it into manageable pieces. Add a touch of butter/oil and herb salt to taste.

1 pound garden spinach
Butter/oil, to taste
Herb salt, to taste

Spinach was a vegetable that Miss O'Keeffe could eat three times a day. One favorite summer breakfast was a poached egg on a bed of steamed spinach, often known as Eggs Florentine.

Eggs Florentine

Spinach
1 egg per serving
Herb salt, to taste
Freshly ground pepper, to taste
Radishes,
    as accompaniment
Whole wheat toast, as accompaniment

For this dish, butter a shallow poaching cup, add the egg, and poach it for 5 minutes, or to taste. While the egg is poaching, add the spinach to a simmering steamer for 3–4 minutes. When the spinach is done, arrange ½ cup or more on a warmed plate, cut it into slightly smaller pieces, then put the poached egg on top. Season with herb salt and freshly ground pepper to taste. Serve crisp, sweet radishes and whole wheat toast on the side.

Miss O'Keeffe would occasionally recount her first New Mexico summers. Before she lived at Ghost Ranch or owned the Abiquiu house, she rented a room in a large ranch house in Alcalde, along the east side of the Rio Grande Valley. She described her work habits at that time: "I would wake up early and be in Abiquiu by eight. I worked very hard—for about two weeks. Then I'd take a trip. That's how I saw most of this country," she said. "But the roads in Kansas were a menace at first—all dirt, and when it rained, there was mud. Everyone got stuck in Kansas. I didn't drive through Kansas until the roads were paved," she commented.

Snow Peas

Select approximately 5 ounces of snow peas per person. Pick only the tender, young pods, which have no tough "strings," or remove any tough strings from each side of the pea. Wash the peas and dry them. Heat a large stainless steel or iron frying pan and add the oil. When the oil is hot, add the snow peas and sauté on medium heat for 3–4 minutes, or to taste. Add a touch of butter/oil and herb salt. Serves 3.

Snow peas are also delectable raw in salads or stir-fried in a wok with vegetables and/or meat.

1 pound snow peas
1–2 tablespoons oil
Butter/oil, to taste
Herb salt, to taste

Beet Greens, Chard, or Turnip Greens

One evening at supper, Miss O'Keeffe told of the day's visitors who had once sent her a Christmas card of them and an elephant they had shot. "I would be ashamed. Elephants are precious," Miss O'Keeffe remarked. She said that she had seen elephants in Ceylon and in the circus—in the circus, with a dingy rose-colored skirt around their backs.

Miss O'Keeffe recalled that once in New York, a friend had come rushing into the Stieglitz and O'Keeffe apartment, having just seen elephants in a parade. "Georgia," he said, "why haven't you ever painted an elephant?" "Because I'm not around them enough, I guess, and I couldn't enlarge them," she replied, referring to her large flower paintings. "Did he think I wasn't kidding?!" she added.

2–4 leaves per serving
Butter/oil, to taste
Herb salt, to taste
½ onion, diced (optional)

Cut tender, medium-sized greens near the bottom of the stems. Wash them, then cut into the leaves to remove the stems. Dry the greens and set the beet or chard stems aside (turnip greens stems can be discarded). Bring a large steamer to a boil, then place the leaves inside and cover. Steam for 5 minutes for beet greens and chard—slightly longer for turnip greens.

To steam the beet green stems, first cut them into 3-inch lengths. Chard stems may be cut in halves or thirds lengthwise, then cut into 3-inch segments. Put the stems in the steamer 5–7 minutes before the leaves are added, so that the stalks can steam for 10–12 minutes in all. Two varieties of chard grew in the garden: red and green. The red chard stems were usually slightly sweeter than the green stems.

The beet and chard stems have a slightly different flavor than the leaves and can be mixed with the steamed leaves or presented as a separate vegetable. Serve the slightly chopped greens and/or stems on a warmed plate with butter/oil and herb salt to taste.

These greens and stems can also be sautéed in oil (safflower, peanut, olive, sunflower, etc.). Once again, the stems should be added 5–7 minutes before the leaves. Half of a small onion, diced, adds extra flavor to the sautéed greens.

One rather unusual taste is the sour/sweet flavor of green tomatoes when they are cooked with onion and a little sugar. If a few tomatoes were large, but had not yet turned red, this was a delicious way to use that fruit.

Fried Green Tomatoes

Peel the tomatoes by scalding them in boiling water for 30 seconds, or by holding them over a gas flame with a fork. Slice the peeled tomatoes about ½-inch thick. Slice the onion ¼-inch thick. Heat an iron frying pan and add the butter/oil to the pan. Sauté the onion in the fat on a low heat until it begins to turn translucent. Then add the sliced tomatoes to the pan. Stir the onions and tomatoes together, add the sugar, and cook 3 or 4 minutes, or until the tomatoes are tender. Add herb salt to taste. Serves 2.

2 medium green tomatoes
½ medium onion
1 tablespoon butter/oil
Pinch of sugar
Herb salt, to taste

Verdolaga (Purslane)

Verdolaga, or purslane, is a fleshy annual that quickly spread across the country after it was brought to the New World by early travelers. The plant is native to India and Africa and was introduced to Europeans as a salad plant during the fifteenth century. Its medicinal uses included treatment for fevers and inflammations.

This herb was cultivated by the early settlers primarily for use in salads. It is highly nutritious, containing quantities of calcium, phosphorous, and iron.

2 bunches verdolaga
2 strips bacon
2 tablespoons oil
3 tablespoons onion, diced
Herb salt, to taste

Leaving the stems intact, wash the greens carefully to remove all fine dirt or sand. Dry the verdolaga and cut off any tough stem ends. Then chop it into 1½-inch pieces. Heat a medium-sized frying pan and cook the bacon until it is done, but not crisp. Remove the bacon and chop it roughly. Add the oil to the bacon fat and return the pan to the heat. When the oil is hot, sauté the onion and verdolaga for 7–10 minutes, or until the vegetable is tender. Add the bacon and herb salt during the last few minutes of cooking. Serves 3–4.

As well as eating many vegetables prepared in a nutritious way, Miss O'Keeffe exercised daily. She began many a morning by doing a set of exercises recommended for her by her friend Ida Rolf, who developed the Rolfing method; this technique was intended to improve the structural alignment of the body through manipulation of body tissue. The two women had been friends in New York in the 1940s and had sustained their friendship until Rolf's death in 1979.

Green Peas

Bring ½ cup of water to boil. Add the peas and simmer on low heat for 5–7 minutes, or until the peas are tender. While the peas are cooking, sauté the onion with the herb salt in the butter/oil. Drain the peas and add the sautéed onion. Add extra butter/oil, if preferred, and garnish the peas with a pinch of finely chopped parsley. Serves 2.

½ cup water
8 ounces small green peas
1 tablespoon minced onion
1 tablespoon butter/oil
2–3 sprigs finely chopped fresh parsley
Herb salt, to taste

Some summer evenings, Miss O'Keeffe came to the kitchen while supper was being prepared. At times, she put on a certain apron—rick-rack in three colors on a calico print—made by a friend. She said the apron felt like an "ornament," but she wore it nonetheless when she snapped the green beans or shelled the peas.

Green Beans

12 ounces green, purple,
   or yellow beans
10 or more cardamom
   seeds
Butter/oil, to taste
Herb salt, to taste

Choose slender, young beans and wash them. Snap or cut off the ends and snap or cut the beans into pieces about 1-inch long. Boil them for 8–10 minutes, or until they are tender. Drain the water, then set the beans aside with the lid on. Select 10 or more cardamom seeds and grind them to a medium-fine powder with a mortar and pestle. Add this powder to the green beans, along with butter/oil and herb salt to taste. Serves 2–3.

The cardamom, often used in Eastern cuisine, transforms green beans into a rather exotic-tasting vegetable. These beans go well in a menu with Tomato Aspic (p. 6), Cucumber Soup (p. 19), Garlic Sandwiches (p. 79), and fresh peaches with Wheat Germ Bars (p. 98).

While walking through the garden one late afternoon, Miss O'Keeffe told the story of her past arguments with the gardener concerning the most productive spacing for the carrots and planting methods for the corn. The gardener's traditional methods and Miss O'Keeffe's ideas were quite different. Evidently, the two disagreed every year, but the painter admitted, "I usually won."

Carrots

Wash, peel and cut the tough ends off the carrots, then slice them lengthwise into 4 long strips. Cut the lengths again into 1½- to 2-inch segments. When the steamer is simmering, add the carrots and steam for 6 minutes, or until the carrots are adequately tender. Serve with a touch of butter/oil and herb salt to taste. Garnish with finely chopped dill, parsley, or chives.

4 medium carrots
Butter/oil, to taste
Herb salt, to taste
Fresh dill, parsley, or
   chives, as garnish

Stewed Tomatoes with Onion and Green Pepper

Garden tomatoes are a flavorful addition to any meal, served fresh with a pinch of herb salt or incorporated in the following recipes. One summer evening, I was bringing a basket of Abiquiu tomatoes and other produce to Ghost Ranch. I arrived to find company—two poets—and quite a lot of talk. O'Keeffe remarked, "It's easy to talk about what you're going to do—you can talk yourself right through without really doing anything."

This was one way to use the abundance of garden tomatoes that usually occurred in late August and September. This dish can be served at room temperature as a type of condiment or hot as a side dish. You can virtually taste summer sunshine and natural sweetness in this simple recipe.

4 medium tomatoes
1 medium onion
1 medium bell pepper
1 tablespoon oil (olive oil is particularly suited for this dish)
Herb salt, to taste

Scald the tomatoes in boiling water. Peel them and quarter them. Remove the cores and as many seeds as possible. Put the tomatoes in a bowl and set them aside.

Cut the onion into strips ¼-inch wide and 1-inch long. Core the pepper and cut strips the same size. Sauté these two vegetables in the oil until they are nearly tender. Set the vegetables aside.

In a small saucepan, combine the tomatoes, onion, and bell pepper. Bring these to a simmer and season with herb salt. Simmer the vegetables for 10 minutes. Serve in a small bowl as a side vegetable or as a condiment. This dish can also be canned.

Adelle Davis, nutritionist and author, was a definite influence on Miss O'Keeffe's approach to healthy food. Ms. Davis wrote her first books on nutrition and health in the late 1940s. She was recognized for her emphasis on vitamins, minerals, and food balances required in a healthy diet. In her cookbook *Let's Cook It Right,* she described the benefits of natural foods and explained cooking methods that would retain maximum food values.

Broccoli

Cut the broccoli florets from the main stalk. Wash them and cut off the toughest lower part of the stems. Slice the broccoli into halves or quarters lengthwise. When the steamer is simmering, add the broccoli; steam for 5–8 minutes, or until the broccoli is sufficiently tender. Serves 2.

This can be served with a touch of butter/oil and herb salt. It is also very good with the following simple Hollandaise Sauce inspired by Adelle Davis.

4 broccoli florets
Butter/oil, to taste
Herb salt, to taste

Hollandaise Sauce

In a small saucepan, use a whisk to combine the egg yolk, lemon juice, herb salt, and a dash of pepper. When these are thoroughly combined, put the pan on low heat and add the butter/oil in two stages, stirring constantly. When the sauce thickens, remove it from the heat immediately. Serve at once, over broccoli or other preferred vegetable.

1 egg yolk
1 tablespoon lemon juice
¼ teaspoon herb salt
Freshly ground pepper, to taste
4 tablespoons butter/oil

Green Chile with Garlic and Oil

Every summer, there was an abundance of mild green chile grown in the garden. This vegetable could accompany any meal, contributing a gliding texture and mildly hot flavor between bites of tamer foods.

Green chile, a vegetable high in vitamins A and C, is a staple of traditional New Mexican cooking. It is included in many local foods, such as *chile rellenos* (stuffed and fried peppers), green chile enchiladas (corn tortillas filled with cheese and chile, sauced, and baked), and green chile stew. These chiles are becoming more frequently available in markets throughout the country, especially in their canned form. They are sometimes difficult or impossible to find fresh, except in the Southwest.

---

4 or 5 long, healthy green chiles
1–2 teaspoons oil
1–2 garlic cloves
Herb salt, to taste

Roast the chiles under the broiler—rotating until all sides are slightly blackened and the skin is bubbling and separating from the flesh. Then place the chiles in a pan with a tight-fitting lid, or wrap them in wet paper towels. After 15–30 minutes, the skin should easily separate from the flesh. Separate the green/black slightly transparent skin from the chiles. Then slit the chiles lengthwise and remove the white seeds and the 3 or 4 major "veins" inside, as much of the hotness comes from these parts of the pepper. Remove the tough top stem section as well. Be particularly careful not to rub your eyes after handling chiles.

Cut each chile lengthwise into 3 or 4 sections. Arrange these sections on a plate so that they do not overlap. Peel 1 or 2 garlic cloves and crush them over the chiles with a garlic press. Spread the tiny garlic bits evenly over the chile strips. Then pour 1–2 teaspoons of oil over the chile and garlic. Dust lightly with herb salt.

Fried flowers are the most unusual food I ever fixed for Miss O'Keeffe. In early summer, the locust blossoms hung over the adobe wall, so we were able to stop and smell them during our daily walks. One warm afternoon while we were walking, I remarked that most of the people I admired in the Abiquiu area were women. Miss O'Keeffe retorted, "Don't you think it might be that way in the *world?*" She continued, "But don't even breathe it."

Fried Flowers

Pick two locust sprigs, no more than 4 or 5 inches long. Wash them and pat or spin them dry. In a medium-sized mixing bowl, beat the egg white until stiff. In a separate bowl, combine the egg yolk, milk, flour, and salt. Stir until they are smooth. Fold this liquid into the egg white. Set the batter aside.

In a heavy saucepan, melt the butter/oil over a low flame. Gently dip one locust sprig into the batter and lightly coat the flowers. When the butter/oil is gently bubbling, place 1 sprig in the pan and lightly brown that section of flowers. Rotate the flowers in the pan until all sides of the locust are golden brown. Repeat this process with the second sprig. Serve immediately on a warmed plate, with a little maple syrup or honey, if desired.

2 blooming locust sprigs
1 egg, separated
1½ tablespoons milk
1 tablespoon
    unbleached flour
Dash of salt
2 tablespoons butter/oil
Maple syrup or honey, to
    taste, as a topping

Fresh sweet corn is a delight! We could pick the corn, shuck it, boil it, and eat it within minutes. Miss O'Keeffe told stories about Alfred Stieglitz's large family and summer meals at Lake George in New York: "Can you imagine thirty of them sitting around the big table eating corn on the cob?" she said.

Corn on the Cob

4 ears sweet corn
Butter/oil, to taste
Herb salt, to taste
Pepper, to taste

Choose healthy ears of corn with tender kernels. Shuck the corn and cut out any blemishes. Bring 1 quart of water to a boil and add the corn. Boil for 5–8 minutes, or until the corn is tender.

Remove the corn with tongs. Insert pronged corn holders into each end, if preferred. Add butter, herb salt, and pepper to taste.

Note: Fresh corn was frozen for winter use. The ears were partially husked, boiled for 3 or 4 minutes, then sealed in plastic bags. Before cooking with it, the corn was boiled for 4 or 5 minutes, then added to a specific recipe such as Corn Soup (p.23).

After supper at Ghost Ranch, we might sit on the patio and talk as the daylight grew dim. The sagebrush thriving between the flagstones lost its color, and the wooden ladder to the roof faded slightly into the dusk. Miss O'Keeffe told of how she had previously kept a bed on her roof. A rubber sheet protected it from the rain. She had many fond memories of sleeping in her bed under the stars.

Zucchini

Wash the zucchini and cut off the stems. You may also peel it, if you like. Slice the zucchini into 4 segments lengthwise, then chop those segments into pieces ¼-inch wide. Heat an iron or stainless steel frying pan, add the oil, and cook the zucchini and onion on low heat for 8–10 minutes, or to desired tenderness. Stir in the marjoram or summer savory during the last few minutes of cooking. Add herb salt to taste. Serves 3–4.

Chopped tomatoes and green pepper are a colorful addition to this vegetable. Minced garlic can be added for stronger flavor.

2 medium zucchini
4 tablespoons diced
    onion
2 tablespoons oil
1 teaspoon chopped
    fresh marjoram, or ½
    teaspoon chopped
    fresh summer savory
Herb salt, to taste

Turnips

The garden yielded many mild, sweet turnips—crisp and delicious even when eaten raw. Miss O'Keeffe never tired of a flavorful vegetable prepared simply. Similarly, she often favored a simple, consistent style of clothing. If she found a comfortable dress that was easy to wear and had pockets, she would have five or six dresses sewn just like that one. If she found a comfortable, well-made pair of shoes, she would buy several pairs of them. Miss O'Keeffe almost always wore white dresses in the summer and black dresses in the winter. At times she wore black slacks, or a skirt with a suit jacket. At all times, she was well-groomed and neatly dressed and wore the brooch with her initials "GOK" designed by Alexander Calder.

---

3 medium turnips
Butter/oil, to taste
Herb salt, to taste
Freshly ground pepper, to
taste

Select firm, medium-sized turnips, wash them and peel them. Slice them in half, then into pieces ¼-inch thick. Prepare a steamer; when it is simmering, steam the turnips for 5 minutes, or to desired tenderness. Serve with butter/oil, a touch of herb salt, and freshly ground pepper. Serves 3–4.

One frequent topic of conversation during supper was the artist's life in New York. Miss O'Keeffe said there was a prostitute across town who had her same name. People often called one of them for the other. "Once in a while, we'd call each other up and laugh about it," she said with a chuckle.

Beets

Choose firm, medium-sized beets and cut off the beet greens for later use. (See Beet Greens, p. 38) Cut off the roots, and all of the stem section. Wash the beets well, then cut them in half (or in quarters if the beets are large). Boil the beets for 20–30 minutes, or until tender. Pour the water off the beets and cool them slightly; the peels will slide off easily with the help of a paring knife. Slice the beets no more than ⅜-inch thick, into bite-size pieces. Serve on a warmed plate with a bit of butter/oil and herb salt to taste. This vegetable is also tasty when garnished with chopped parsley or chives.

3 or 4 medium beets
Butter/oil, to taste
Herb salt, to taste
Parsley or chives, as garnish

Kale

Miss O'Keeffe had developed many healthy eating habits by the age of ninety. Speaking about age, she commented: "Twenty-five is nothing—it slips right under your feet. A man is at his best at fifty—he's still strong and has learned a good many things." Speaking about herself, she admitted, "I used to think ninety was far away." "Do you think one hundred is far away?" I asked. "Not as far away as I used to—I think I'll make it there," she said.

2–3 kale leaves
Butter/oil, to taste
Herb salt, to taste

Wash the kale leaves carefully, as there are many tiny crevices in this wrinkled vegetable. Remove the stems and any particularly tough ribs. Then chop the kale into thin strips ¼-inch wide and about 2 inches long. Prepare a steamer, add the kale, and cover. Steam for 5–10 minutes, or until the kale is tender enough to enjoy. Serve with butter/oil and herb salt to taste. Serves 2–3.

This is a slightly chewy vegetable. It has a deep, musky flavor and contains a hefty amount of vitamins A and C, as well as calcium. Suggested menu: Kale, Chicken Soup (p. 31), Irish Soda Bread (p. 77), and Norwegian Apple Pie Cake (p. 97).

In October, as nights began to get cooler, we would need more blankets or quilts on the beds. Miss O'Keeffe owned a very bright red quilt—a contrast to the white and black that filled most of her interior world. An Abiquiu friend had made the quilt, although at first she would have nothing to do with making one. After some time, the friend asked what color Miss O'Keeffe wanted the quilt. "Red," responded the painter. "Oh, certainly I'll make a red one—I thought you just wanted another of those old black things," the friend exclaimed.

Acorn Squash

Preheat the oven to 450°. Wash the squash and cut it in half or quarters. Remove the seeds. Coat the flesh and skin lightly with oil. Add a small pat of butter/oil and a sprinkling of herb salt inside each section. Bake, uncovered, for 45 minutes, or until the flesh is completely tender. Serve with butter/oil, herb salt, and pepper. For additional sweetness, a touch of brown sugar can also be added to the squash during baking. Serves 2.

1 acorn squash
Oil
Butter/oil, to taste
Herb salt, to taste
Brown sugar (optional)
Freshly ground pepper, to
    taste

Fried Potatoes

One particularly prized breakfast treat was fried potatoes. Leftover baked potatoes were used to make this simple dish. After breakfast one morning, I asked Miss O'Keeffe why she did not go to an honorary ceremony for women artists held by President Carter that month in Washington. "Could you imagine—all sitting on a platform—a lot of just women?" she asked. "I've done it too often. Those days are over," she stated firmly.

2 leftover baked Idaho, Russet, or sweet potatoes
½ small white or yellow onion
2 tablespoons oil
Herb salt, to taste
Freshly ground pepper, to taste
Chopped parsley

Cut the potatoes into slices about ¼-inch thick, keeping the skins on if possible. Cut the onion the same thickness. Heat the oil in an iron frying pan. When it is hot, add the onions and gently sauté for about 3 minutes. Then add the potatoes, distributing them evenly to brown all slices. When the onions are translucent and the potatoes are somewhat golden brown on both sides, stir in some finely chopped parsley. Before serving, add a touch of herb salt and freshly ground pepper to taste. Serves 2.

Leftover sweet potatoes can be fried in this same manner, omitting the onions; however, sweet potatoes have a delicate consistency, so care must be taken in turning them. They also have a high sugar content and burn easily, so watch them during cooking.

This was a special dish, which Miss O'Keeffe would often request providing the dandelions were young and tender. Dandelion greens were some of the earliest edible plants to appear in the garden each year. They contain a large amount of vitamins A, B1, and B2. They also contribute calcium, potassium, and iron. The leaves should be picked while they are still quite small or they will be bitter. It is advisable to blanch these greens before serving them in salads or as a vegetable.

Dandelion roots are used medicinally as a mild laxative, blood cleanser, and tonic. In Chinese medicine, they are ground and used as a poultice for snake bites.

Mashed Potatoes with Dandelion Greens

Heat the water to boiling in a heavy 2-quart pan. While the water is heating, peel the potatoes and cut them into quarters. After about 20 minutes, or when the potatoes are tender, drain the cooking water from the potatoes. With a heavy potato masher, mash the potatoes, using 2 tablespoons of butter/oil and ¼ cup of the milk. After the potatoes are mashed to a smooth consistency, add more butter/oil and/or milk if necessary. Then incorporate the dandelion greens, stirring well to mix them into the potatoes. Add herb salt and freshly ground pepper to taste.

6–8 fine-grained potatoes
½ cup or more of roughly chopped young, tender dandelion greens
2–4 tablespoons of butter/oil
½ cup milk, or to taste
Herb salt, to taste
Freshly ground pepper, to taste

main dishes

Various types of meat were often served with the noon meal, although meat was not considered a daily necessity. This meal was generally the most substantial of the day, often including a salad, one or two vegetables, potatoes or rice, the main dish, and a dessert.

Baked Chicken with Lemon

If company was coming, and we did not have much notice, this was a frequent choice for the main course. At the high baking temperature, the chicken was cooked thoroughly and was quite tender. The lemon and salt used in the following recipe permeated the meat and made it unusually good. Leaving the chicken uncovered for the final ten minutes gave the skin a beautiful golden color. This is a simple, fast, and delicious way to cook chicken.

During the noontime conversation one weekend, Miss O'Keeffe recounted life at her Ghost Ranch house in the 1940s. "If I couldn't get along out here by myself, I wasn't worth much," she told me. She described one of her habits at that time: "I wouldn't even wash the dishes if I didn't want to. Sometimes I had them stacked all along that counter at the ranch, but I knew a time would come when I'd do them; I wasn't going to wash the dishes if I had other big things to do."

1 3–4 pound chicken
2 fresh lemons
1 teaspoon Kosher salt
2 garlic cloves

Preheat the oven to 400°. Wash the chicken and cut off the excess fat. Pat the chicken dry inside and outside, then place it in a glass or metal baking pan or a covered casserole dish. Cut the 2 lemons in half, then squeeze the halves from 1 lemon to distribute juice inside the cavity; squeeze the remaining halves on the skin. Rub ½ teaspoon of salt inside the chicken cavity and the other ½ teaspoon over the chicken skin. Peel the garlic cloves and cut them in half. Put 2 halves inside the chicken and the other 2 halves in the pan.

Seal the pan with a cover of aluminum foil and place the chicken in the oven. After 45 minutes, remove the foil and bake for another 15 minutes. This should brown the skin nicely. If additional browning is necessary, turn the oven setting to "broil" for 1–2 minutes.

Carve the chicken into slices, keeping the drumsticks and wings whole. Serve from a platter or prepare individual plates. Leftover chicken can be used in Curried Chicken (p. 59) or added to Chicken Soup (p. 31). Serves 3–4.

Miss O'Keeffe continued to paint in acrylic and watercolor and to work with clay in her early nineties. Along with these pursuits, she also wrote short essays on certain themes: her dogs, her dreams, and the people she had known. She had written a number of pieces on her personal reflections over the forty-five years she had lived in Abiquiu—all in her distinctive style, which took great liberty with phrasing and punctuation.

Many years previously, she had written an article about Alfred Stieglitz for the *New York Times*. "They took my writing and changed it to proper English, like anyone would write," she said. "I told them they shouldn't print it if they didn't do it exactly the way I wrote it." She continued, "Of course, they changed it back."

Curried Chicken

In a medium-sized frying pan, melt 1 tablespoon of the butter/oil over low heat. Add the onion and celery and sauté until transparent. Remove those vegetables from the pan and set them aside. Add the second tablespoon of butter/oil to the pan. Then add 1 tablespoon of whole wheat flour. Stir with a whisk until the two ingredients have blended into a roux and are gently bubbling. Slowly add the milk, stirring with the whisk to keep the mixture smooth. When the milk has become the consistency of heavy cream, add the onion, celery, egg, chicken, and curry powder. Let the curry simmer for 5 minutes, or until the ingredients are thoroughly heated. Serve over Brown Rice with Ginger (p. 89). Garnish with fresh parsley. Serves 3.

Finely diced red or green pepper, or fresh green peas, can also be added in the initial steps of this recipe. Add the curry powder to taste—more may be desired.

2 tablespoons butter/oil
½ onion, finely diced
1 stalk celery, finely diced
1 tablespoon whole wheat flour
1 cup milk
1 hard-boiled egg, roughly chopped
½ to 1 cup leftover chicken cut in ½-inch chunks
1 teaspoon mild curry powder, or to taste
Herb salt, to taste
Parsley, as garnish
Red or green pepper, diced (optional)
½ cup green peas (optional)

Broiled T-Bone Steak

A thick, juicy steak was prepared every week or two. Miss O'Keeffe did eat red meat in moderation, usually with the noon meal. This meat was always ordered from a particular Santa Fe market. Every few weeks, one of Miss O'Keeffe's staff would make the trip "to town" for all needed supplies, including thick, high-quality T-bone steak, cubes of sirloin steak for stew, twice-ground round steak, chicken, and for special occasions, a leg of lamb.

1 16-ounce T-bone steak, 1½-inches thick
¼ cup Herb Salad Dressing, containing 1 extra minced garlic clove
Parsley, as garnish

Take the steak out of the refrigerator 1 hour before broiling. Prick both sides of the meat several times with a fork, then put it on a large, shallow platter. Pour the dressing over the steak and turn it once so that the top side has a thin coat of oil, garlic, and herbs. The steak should marinate in the dressing for 30 minutes per side. It can marinate, covered, at room temperature, or in the refrigerator if preferred.

After the steak has marinated, preheat the broiler for 5 minutes. Drain some of the excess dressing before placing the steak on the broiler. Cook the meat for about 5 minutes on each side, or to taste. Serve on a warmed plate, garnished with parsley.

Before the noon meal one Saturday, we were reading a magazine article entitled "The Scientific Pursuit of Happiness." "I think it's so foolish for people to want to be happy," Miss O'Keeffe said. "Happiness is so momentary—you're happy for an instant and then you start thinking again," she remarked. She continued, "Interest is the most important thing in life; happiness is temporary, but interest is continuous."

Beef Stew

In a large, heavy saucepan, brown the beef in the oil. Then cover the meat with water or beef stock, place a tight-fitting lid over the saucepan, and simmer for 2–3 hours, or until the meat is tender. After 2 hours, add the carrots, potatoes, onions, lovage, bay leaf, and garlic to the pot. After 2½ hours, check the tenderness of the meat and vegetables and season with the desired amount of salt and freshly ground pepper.

To thicken the stew slightly, take 2 tablespoons of the simmering liquid from the pot and combine it until smooth with 1 teaspoon of flour. Return this thickener to the pot and rapidly stir it into the liquid. Serve on warmed plates. Serves 2–3.

1 pound beef sirloin tip, or other tender cut trimmed of most fat and cut into 1–1½-inch cubes
1 tablespoon oil
Water or beef stock
3 carrots, peeled and cut into ¾-inch chunks
2 medium potatoes, scrubbed and cut into ¾-inch chunks
½ onion, chopped into ½-inch chunks
2 small lovage sprigs
1 bay leaf
2 garlic cloves, cut in half
Herb salt, to taste
Freshly ground pepper, to taste
1 teaspoon flour, optional

Meatloaf

This is a dish I remember making for lunch at Ghost Ranch. In the summer, when breezes blew through the patio, I could hear the soft, deep, and resonant sound of a round, three-foot-wide steel sawblade that Miss O'Keeffe had nailed to her adobe wall. There was also a small, high-pitched bell that hung near her studio door. Other sounds were the ravens calling as they soared on the updrafts near the cliffs. Outside the window by the small kitchen table, the piñon trees swayed gracefully, and Miss O'Keeffe observed that she could see the trees "breathing."

1 pound lean, twice-ground round steak
½ cup soft breadcrumbs from homemade whole wheat bread
2 garlic cloves, minced
4–5 leaves fresh lovage, finely chopped
4–5 fresh celery leaves, finely chopped
½ onion, finely chopped
½ teaspoon herb salt
1 egg, slightly beaten
¼ cup milk
¼ cup home-canned tomato sauce, or high-quality commercial sauce

Preheat the oven to 350°. In a large mixing bowl, combine the ground round steak with all the dry ingredients so that they are distributed evenly. Next, lightly beat the egg in a small bowl and mix it into the meat mixture. Finally, add the milk and blend into the meat mixture. Shape the mixture into a loaf and place it in a greased baking pan. Pour the tomato sauce on top of the meatloaf. Bake the meat for 1 hour. Slice the loaf and serve it on warmed plates. Serves 6.

This keeps well as a leftover. Suggested menus: Meatloaf (p. 62), steamed Spinach (p. 35), baked potatoes, Beet and Green Bean Salad (p. 5), and Applesauce (p. 95).

This recipe can also be adapted for meatballs. More herbs can be added to the meat—a bit of finely chopped fresh (or ground dried) rosemary, ½ teaspoon of summer savory, 1 tablespoon of chopped parsley, or any combination to taste. Shape the meatballs into 1- to 1½-inch rounds. Cook them with oil in an iron frying pan over low heat, turning them frequently so that all sides are browned. Then add a lid and cook on low heat for 5 minutes, or until sufficiently done. Serves 6.

This was a festive dish, served occasionally on holidays or when special company arrived. At Easter, Thanksgiving, or Christmas, there was often a special meal at the Abiquiu house for Miss O'Keeffe, her business manager, and a few friends. For an Easter feast, we served the following dish with the Honey Mint Sauce below, Mashed Potatoes with Dandelion Greens (p. 55), Classic Summer Salad (p. 2), steamed Carrots (p. 43), and White Fruit Cake (p. 101).

Roast Leg of Lamb with Garlic

Preheat the oven to 325°. With a small, very sharp knife, make slits about 1 inch apart over the entire meaty section of the lamb. The slits should be about ⅜-inch deep. Into each slit, stuff 1 garlic slice. (This is quite a time-consuming task.) Place the lamb on a rack in a shallow roasting pan, without a cover. Add salt and pepper. Roast 15–20 minutes per pound. When the meat is done, place it on a heated serving platter and carve it at the table. Serve with Honey Mint Sauce. Serves 5–7.

1 leg of lamb (6–7 pounds)
4–5 garlic cloves cut in halves or thirds, in thin slices
Salt, to taste
Pepper, to taste

Honey Mint Sauce

Warm the honey and vinegar on low heat in a small saucepan. Stir until the liquid is well blended, then pour it over the mint. Cool the sauce to room temperature. Serve from a small pitcher or bowl as an accompaniment to the lamb.

½ cup honey
2 tablespoons apple cider vinegar
½ cup mint, finely chopped

Herbed Thanksgiving Stuffing

for a 16-pound turkey

6 cups homemade whole
  wheat bread crumbs
  (or combination white
  and wheat)
1 cup celery, chopped
1½ cups onion, diced
3 tablespoons safflower oil
¼ cup loosely packed
  chopped celery leaves
¼ cup loosely packed
  chopped parsley
3 tablespoons minced
  fresh sage leaves
3 tablespoons chopped
  lovage
1–2 teaspoons minced
  thyme leaves
1 teaspoon powdered
  marjoram
1 to 1½ cups chicken broth
½ cup butter/oil
1 teaspoon herb salt, or to
  taste
Freshly ground pepper, to
  taste

One Thanksgiving, Miss O'Keeffe had said we would prepare the turkey for a group of young friends. We set the alarm for 4:45 a.m. In the dark, we headed to the kitchen to stuff the turkey. Miss O'Keeffe donned a white chef's apron over her robe and stirred the dressing made the previous evening. I stuffed the twenty-pound bird, then skewered it closed. As the household oven was too small for this large turkey, Miss O'Keeffe had arranged to have it roasted by a friend in a house nearby. We drove while it was still very dark to deliver the turkey to the appropriate oven. Then we returned to the house for an early breakfast by the fire, and vocal music of Monteverdi. By early afternoon, the turkey was collected and taken to the Thanksgiving party where it was greatly admired then prompty eaten.

Dry several slices of homemade whole wheat (or white and wheat) bread. Break dried bread into pieces and put these in a paper bag; roll over these with a heavy rolling pin to make pea-sized pieces along with finer crumbs. Put the breadcrumbs into a large mixing bowl. Sauté the celery and onions in 3 tablespoons safflower oil until soft but not brown. Add the vegetables to the bread crumbs and mix. Add the chopped celery leaves and herbs. Finally, add the chicken broth, 1 cup at first, and lightly stir to mix. Then add the butter/oil and do the same. If stuffing does not have enough liquid, add more chicken broth. Salt and pepper to taste. Add more herbs to taste if necessary. Loosely spoon the stuffing into the front cavity and skewer or sew the turkey skin together to seal the opening.

Miss O'Keeffe thought that liver was a good food to eat occasionally, but that the only way it was palatable was to soak it in milk first. She said that the milk subdued the strong liver flavor. Miss O'Keeffe developed several habits that she practiced because she thought they were good for her. After breakfast in the morning, she often took a tablespoon of brewer's yeast mixed into ¼ cup of water, followed by a tablespoon of molasses. Once a day, she took one tablespoon of lecithin mixed with water, and seaweed agar was also taken in water.

Liver and Onions

Wash the liver and pat it dry; trim the tough outer membrane and any inner membranes from each piece. Pour the milk into a large shallow bowl and soak the liver in it. Make sure the milk totally covers the liver. Soak the liver in the milk for 1 hour.

After that time, heat 2 tablespoons of oil in a large iron skillet. When the skillet is hot, gently sauté the onion until it is nearly transparent. At that point, move the onion to the edges of the skillet and add the third tablespoon of oil, then add the liver. Cook the liver 3–4 minutes on each side, or to taste. Serves 2.

Serve with Classic Summer Salad (p. 2), baked potato, Beet Greens (p. 38), and Vanilla Rennet Custard (p. 94).

½ pound fresh beef liver
1 cup milk
3 tablespoons oil
1 medium onion, sliced
   in ⅜-inch pieces
Herb salt, to taste
Freshly ground pepper, to
   taste

Spinach Quiche

Miss O'Keeffe was interested in a wide range of books, evidenced by selections that I read with her. *The Ascent of Man* by Jacob Bronowski, *Of Kennedy and Kings* by Gerald Dickler, and Loren Eiseley's *The Immense Journey* were a few titles. *The Letters of Henry Miller and Wallace Fowlie, Letters to a Disciple* about Mahatma Gandhi, and *The Rodale Herb Book* were other books she enjoyed. At Ghost Ranch and in Abiquiu, there was a "book room" filled with many titles that had been read and enjoyed.

8 ounces fresh spinach
½ medium onion, finely diced
1 tablespoon butter/oil
3 eggs
1½ cups whole milk
1 cup grated cheddar cheese
¼ teaspoon herb salt
Freshly ground pepper, to taste
One Whole Wheat Pastry Flour Crust (p. 67)

Preheat the oven to 450°. Wash the spinach well to remove all fine sand. Spin or pat it dry, then roughly chop it. Dice the onion. Heat a large frying pan and add the butter/oil. When the oil mixture bubbles, add the onion and sauté until it is translucent. Add the chopped spinach to the onion and cook it for 2 or 3 minutes, or until the spinach has collapsed and is tender. Remove the vegetables from the pan and set them aside.

Break the 3 eggs into a large mixing bowl and stir with a fork to blend them. Add the milk, cheese, salt, and a little freshly ground pepper. Stir to blend these ingredients thoroughly. Then stir the onion and spinach into the mixture.

Pour this liquid into the following pie crust made with whole wheat pastry flour. Bake at 450° for 10 minutes, then turn the temperature down to 350° for 20–30 minutes. Test the quiche at 30 minutes. Serves 6.

Note: The fresh spinach tends to stratify during baking. This quiche is also quite good with green chile. In place of spinach, substitute 1 cup finely chopped mild green chile, roasted and peeled, with seeds and veins removed. This produces a mildly hot and flavorful quiche.

Whole Wheat Pastry Flour Crust

Measure 2 cups of whole wheat pastry flour into a large mixing bowl. Stir the salt into the flour. Cut the oil and butter or shortening into the flour. Blend until the mixture resembles fine crumbs. Add ice water gradually. Add water until the dough will hold together in a ball. Flour a large board and roll out the dough into a thin crust. Gently transfer the dough to a 9-inch baking pan. Trim the edges, leaving enough dough to pinch together and crimp along the side. Pour the quiche liquid into this pastry and bake as described on previous page.

2 cups whole wheat pastry flour, or 1 cup each whole wheat flour and unbleached flour
¼ teaspoon herb salt
2 tablespoons safflower oil
4 tablespoons butter or vegetable shortening
4 tablespoons ice water

Herb Omelet

My usual responsibilities in the O'Keeffe household began at 5 p.m. and ended at about 8:30 a.m., and included several weekends. In the morning when I left, Miss O'Keeffe would often say goodbye with a graceful wave of her right hand. "Goodbye—luck to you," she would say. She sometimes commented, "You carry your good times with you. If you don't make your own good time, you might not have it."

2 fresh eggs
1 tablespoon water
2 teaspoons of any rather mild fresh herb, such as dill, thyme, parsley, marjoram, or chives
1 tablespoon butter/oil
Herb salt, to taste
Freshly ground pepper, to taste
Parsley and diced tomatoes, as garnish

Break the 2 eggs into a mixing bowl. Stir with a fork to blend them. Mix in the tablespoon of water. Chop the selected herb rather fine and add it to the eggs. If desired add herb salt and pepper.

Heat a small iron frying pan or omelet pan over a low flame. Melt 1 tablespoon of butter/oil in the pan. When this gently sizzles, add the egg and herb mixture. As the egg cooks, slide a fork or knife around the edges to make sure the sides are not sticking. Keep the heat low so that the egg cooks slowly on the bottom, while also cooking the top. When the bottom is golden brown (lift an edge up slightly with a fork), fold half of the omelet over the other half. Serves 1–2.

An additional generous teaspoon of the herb, finely chopped, can be sautéed in butter and spread over the inside of the omelet. Garnish with diced tomatoes and/or parsley.

During many evening meals, Miss O'Keeffe referred to her previous life in New York with photographer Alfred Stieglitz. "It is as if I have lived many lives," she would say. In remembering Stieglitz, Miss O'Keeffe commented that he loved the "sporting page." "He could tell you anything about sports," she said. "People thought that he liked the arts section, but he cared nothing for that."

Stieglitz also enjoyed the horse races, as did O'Keeffe. She said that the most exciting race she ever saw was at Saratoga, when Man of War was winning. "The people were wonderful to watch, and the racing, as the horses came in front of the audience, was quite thrilling," she said. Miss O'Keeffe also liked "the fights" (boxing). Later, in her travels to Spain, she became quite interested in the bull-fights, although she commented that the sight of the bull's blood "broke me down."

Tomato Soufflé

Preheat the oven to 375°. In a medium saucepan, melt the butter/oil. Add the pastry flour and stir it with a spoon until the mixture forms a roux and is gently sizzling. Then slowly add the tomato sauce, stirring continuously as the sauce thickens. When this mixture is thick and smooth, remove it from the heat and add the cheese, cumin, and salt. Stir to blend it thoroughly, then cool it to room temperature. Next, stir in the egg yolks, one at a time.

Beat the egg whites until stiff peaks form. Fold 1 or 2 tablespoons of the beaten egg whites into the cheese and tomato mixture. Then carefully fold in the remaining egg whites. Spoon this mixture into a well-buttered soufflé dish. Bake for 25 minutes, or until the soufflé has risen and is golden and slightly firm. Serve in wedges, with a bit of freshly ground pepper. Serves 5.

2 tablespoons butter/oil
2 tablespoons whole wheat pastry flour
1 cup homemade tomato sauce, or high-quality canned sauce
1 cup grated cheddar cheese
1 teaspoon whole cumin seeds, ground fine with a mortar and pestle
¼ teaspoon herb salt
4 eggs, separated
Freshly ground pepper, to taste

Tortillas, made of corn or flour, are the traditional Mexican and New Mexican alternative to bread. In these two enchilada recipes, either yellow or blue corn tortillas may be used. Tortillas in frozen form are becoming more widely available across the country as the popularity of New Mexican and Mexican cooking increases. Blue corn meal is ground from a species of blue corn that has been cultivated for centuries in regions of the Southwest.

Green Chile Chicken Enchiladas

1 cup sliced or shredded precooked chicken
¾ cup Monterey Jack or mild cheddar cheese
⅓ cup minced onion
1 tablespoon oil
8 yellow or blue corn tortillas
2 cups green chile sauce (p.71)

Prepare the chicken, grate the cheese, and mince the onion. Heat an iron frying pan and add the oil. Sauté the onion until it is transparent, then set the onions aside and clean the pan. Add a slight amount of oil to the pan and return it to medium heat. When the oil is hot, quickly heat all of the tortillas on both sides so they are soft and pliable, adding more oil as necessary to prevent them from sticking. Keep the tortillas covered until they are used.

Preheat the oven to 350°. For each serving, dip 1 tortilla into the green chile sauce to lightly coat it. Place it on an ovenproof stoneware dish. Add the chicken, onions, and cheese. Then add another tortilla on top and cover it with about ⅓ cup of green chile sauce; spoon this sauce on top of the enchilada so that it completely coats the tortillas. Using a new plate each time, make all 4 servings, then bake the enchiladas for about 10 minutes, or until the chile begins to bubble. In the last few minutes of cooking, add a little grated cheese on top. Serves 4.

Green Chile Sauce

Roast the green chiles in the broiler or over a grill so that the thin outside skin begins to blister and turn black in places. Put the chiles in a covered pan, or inside wet paper towels, so that the skin will loosen easily from the flesh. After 10 to 15 minutes, peel the skin from the chiles. Also, remove the tough tops and stems and the seeds and veins (the seeds and veins tend to be the hottest parts of the chile). Chop the chiles into small pieces. Note: Be very careful not to rub your eyes after handling chiles.

In a small saucepan, melt 1 tablespoon of butter/oil. When the butter is hot, add the onion and sauté until it is transparent. Then add the chicken broth, green chile, and garlic. When the broth is hot, add the cornstarch- or flour-and-water thickener and stir while the sauce thickens. Set the sauce aside while beginning the enchiladas.

1 pound fresh green chiles
1 tablespoon butter/oil
½ onion, chopped fine
2 cups homemade chicken broth, or high-quality canned broth
1 garlic clove, minced
1 tablespoon flour or cornstarch, mixed with 2 tablespoons water

All ingredients for this recipe could be found at Bode's General Store on the main road through Abiquiu. Miss O'Keeffe remembered that the late Martin Bode, of German descent, had stocked good black bread and some very good cheese in her early Abiquiu days.

Red Chile Cheese Enchiladas

1 cup grated Monterey Jack or mild cheddar cheese
¼ cup minced onion
8 yellow or blue corn tortillas
1 tablespoon safflower oil
2 cups red chile sauce

Grate the cheese and mince the onion. Heat an iron frying pan and add the oil. Sauté the onion until it is transparent, then set the onions aside and clean the pan. Add a slight amount of oil to the pan and return it to medium heat. When the oil is hot, quickly heat both sides of the tortillas so that they are soft and pliable, adding more oil as necessary to keep the tortillas from sticking. Keep the tortillas covered until they are used.

Preheat the oven to 350°. For each serving, dip 1 heated tortilla into the red chile sauce to lightly coat it. Then, place it on an ovenproof stoneware dish. Sprinkle 3–4 tablespoons of cheese evenly on top of the tortilla. Then add 1 scant tablespoon of cooked onions. Place another tortilla on top, then cover it with about ⅓ cup of red chile sauce; spoon this sauce on top of the enchilada so that it completely coats the tortillas. Using a new plate each time, do the same thing for all 4 servings, then bake the enchiladas for about 10 minutes, or until the chile begins to bubble. In the last few minutes of cooking, add a little grated cheese on top. Serves 4.

Red Chile Sauce

Remove the chile tops and the dried white seeds. Break the chiles into several pieces and place them in a mixing bowl. Pour boiling water over the chile to cover it, then set it aside, covered, for a few hours or overnight. After that time, put the soaked chile and 2 cups of its liquid in a blender. Add the peeled garlic cloves and ¼ teaspoon of herb salt. Blend at the highest speed for 30 seconds, or until the chile is completely smooth. If necessary, add water to make 2 cups of sauce. The sauce may be strained for extra smoothness. Set the chile aside to begin the enchiladas. Remember not to rub your eyes after handling chiles.

8 or 9 dried whole red
  chiles
Boiling water
1 or 2 garlic cloves
¼ teaspoon herb salt

Posole

Posole is hominy that has been soaked in water with lime. In New Mexico, either fresh-frozen or dried posole is available. One northern New Mexico tradition is to serve posole on Christmas Eve. In Abiquiu many years ago, Miss O'Keeffe described how, on that night, the village people would build bonfires *(luminarias)* and decorate the exteriors of their homes with candles placed inside paper bags *(farolitos)*, then proceed from house to house for posole and other native foods. Miss O'Keeffe recalled that little boys would sometimes have soot on their pants from jumping over those bonfires. In years past, she had opened her house to the community on Christmas Eve and served tamales (shredded meat seasoned with chile, encased in fine cornmeal dough and steamed in cornhusks), posole, and *empanaditas* (meat pies or sweet pies). However, Miss O'Keeffe noted that no posole recipe was completely authentic without pig's knuckles, an item used to flavor and thicken the posole that could be bought in various northern New Mexico markets.

---

3 or 4 country-style pork ribs
Pig's knuckles (optional)
1 chopped onion
1 tablespoon oil
1 package frozen posole, or dried posole soaked overnight and rinsed
2 cups homemade chicken broth or water
2 garlic cloves, cut in half
Fresh or dried oregano, to taste
Herb salt, to taste
Shredded green cabbage (optional garnish)

Heat a large soup kettle. Brown the ribs and pig's knuckles in their own fat, or use 1 extra tablespoon of oil if the ribs are quite lean. While the meat is browning, add the onions and oil. Sauté the onions for about 5 minutes. Add the posole, then add enough water (some chicken broth can be added for richer flavor) to cover the posole with 1 inch of liquid. Add the garlic and a pinch of oregano. Bring the posole to a low simmer and cook 3–4 hours, or until the posole is very tender. Add herb salt to taste. Serves 10.

This soup is delicious when mixed with either Red Chile Sauce (p. 73) or Green Chile Sauce (p. 71). Another variation is to add a touch of finely shredded green cabbage on top.

breads, grains, & cereals

Whole wheat yeast and quick breads, whole grain cereals, and brown rice were staples in the O'Keeffe household. They accompanied most meals in a variety of forms.

Whole Wheat Bread

The flour for this bread (and all recipes containing wheat flour) was always ground with Miss O'Keeffe's small mill in the pantry. She had developed a recipe similar to this one for flavorful, moist bread with a rather fine texture. Quite often this bread was served at breakfast, toasted in her old-fashioned toaster with center heating coils and two hinged metal sides with open grillwork. The toast was browned on one side, then turned so the the center coils would toast the other side.

The whole wheat flour in this recipe should be finely ground. Use of whole wheat pastry flour is not advised since it contains less gluten. Two or three cups of unbleached white flour may be substituted for the whole wheat.

2½ cups milk
1 tablespoon dried yeast
¼ cup warm (110°) water
2 tablespoons honey
2 tablespoons oil
¾ teaspoon salt
6 cups whole wheat flour
½ cup wheat germ

Scald the milk, then cool it to room temperature. In a large mixing bowl, dissolve the yeast in the warm (110°) water with a teaspoon of the honey. Let it stand 5 minutes, or until foamy. Then add the milk, honey, oil, and salt. Stir these to combine slightly. Next, mix in 3 cups of flour, 1 cup at a time, and the wheat germ. Continue to add the flour until the dough is too stiff to stir. Turn the dough out on a floured surface and knead it while adding flour a little at a time until the dough has a workable consistency. Knead until it is smooth and elastic.

Place the dough in an oiled bowl, turning it once so that the bottom surface is on top. Cover the dough with a clean cloth and place it in a warm area. Let the dough rise for 1 hour, or until doubled in bulk.

Preheat the oven to 375°. Punch the dough down and divide it into 2 loaves. Shape the loaves and place them in oiled bread pans. Let the bread rise until almost doubled (about 30 minutes). Bake the loaves for about 45 minutes, or until the base of the loaves sounds hollow when tapped. Remove the bread from the pans and cool on a rack. Store the bread in an airtight container or package. Note: This recipe is designed for high-altitude baking. For lower altitudes, decrease the quantity of milk and bake at 350°.

If we knew company was coming, and we had no bread in the house, Irish Soda Bread was the quick solution. Made from home-ground flour, homemade yogurt, and local honey, this was a delicious accompaniment to soups and salads at supper.

Supper guests were not common, but a friend, or at times family, might be visiting. Infrequently, Miss O'Keeffe's sisters, Claudia and Catherine, would plan to visit "Georgia" at the same time. On one particular occasion, Catherine's daughter also visited. The four related women had very lively conversations during a rather late supper. Afterwards, one of the sisters asked Miss O'Keeffe if they had tired her out. "Certainly not—I feel like the morning star," O'Keeffe replied.

Irish Soda Bread

Preheat the oven to 375°. Beat the yogurt and egg together in a small bowl. Measure the dry ingredients into a large mixing bowl. Make a well in the center, pour in the yogurt-and-egg mixture, and gradually stir into the dry ingredients until they are well combined. Turn the dough out onto a clean, floured surface. Knead it briefly, until it is smooth. Divide the dough into 2 equal pieces. Shape them into slightly flattened rounds. Then place them in oiled or greased pie pans. Make 2 or 3 long, shallow slashes across the tops of the loaves. Bake for 35 minutes. Serve while warm, with butter/oil.

1½ cups yogurt
1 egg
1½ teaspoons baking soda
1 tablespoon baking powder
¾ teaspoon salt
4 cups stone-ground whole wheat flour, or 2 cups whole wheat and 2 cups unbleached flour

Cottage Cheese Herb Bread

Herbs were used in many recipes, as well as in this bread. Dried herbs can be used in this and other recipes, if fresh are not available; however, the dried herbs should be substituted in about half the amount stated for the fresh herbs. During late summer and fall, many garden herbs were tied in bundles and hung from the vigas in the dark pantry to dry. Then the leaves were separated from the stems and were stored in airtight jars. Some jars looked as though they had been used for many seasons throughout the kitchen's three decades of existence. The jars were labeled and placed in the cool, dark pantry for use in many foods and teas.

¼ cup warm (110°) water or milk

1 tablespoon dried yeast

1 tablespoon sugar

1 cup creamy cottage cheese, slightly warmed

2 tablespoons fresh parsley, finely chopped

2 tablespoons finely chopped onion

1 tablespoon oil

1 egg slightly beaten

¾ teaspoon salt

¼ teaspoon baking powder

2¼ cups stone-ground whole wheat flour, or a combination of whole wheat and unbleached flours

Combine the warm water or milk and yeast in a large mixing bowl. Allow the yeast to dissolve completely. Then add the sugar, warm cottage cheese, parsley, onion, oil, and egg, beating well to combine these ingredients thoroughly. Next, add the salt, baking powder, and flour. Beat well for 100 strokes. Place in a well-greased casserole or soufflé dish to rise for 1 hour.

Preheat the oven to 350°. When the bread has risen sufficiently, bake it for 40–50 minutes. Serve warm, with butter/oil.

Other fresh herbs such as dill, sage, or rosemary can be substituted. Coarsely ground caraway seeds also contribute a nice taste.

Written records attest to the use of garlic since 3,000 B.C. It had prominent medicinal use by the Babylonians, the Chinese, and the Egyptians. Recently, garlic has been shown to reduce blood pressure in hypertensive patients, to perform as an antibacterial agent within the body, and to act as an antiseptic for open wounds. It has also been used to combat dizziness and headaches. Garlic has long been used as a remedy for colds, sore throats, and earaches. The herb is also a natural insecticide.

Miss O'Keeffe believed in the virtues of garlic; it was grown in the garden every year. She used the bulb in many forms. She may have invented this direct and surprisingly delicious way of eating raw garlic, served between slices of crusty French bread.

Garlic Sandwiches

Cut 2 rather thin slices of French bread. Butter, or brush with olive oil, each slice to taste. Arrange 2 or 3 garlic slices on one buttered side of French bread. Put the other buttered bread slice on top of the first slice, for the completed garlic sandwich.

1 loaf French bread
Butter/olive oil
1 garlic clove, cut into
    very thin slices

Popovers

Popovers are tricky to make. The type and amount of flour used is crucial. The whole wheat flour should be finely ground and does not need to be sifted. One afternoon at Ghost Ranch, we tried two or three times to make these successfully. Between attempts, we sat on the patio looking past the wrought iron "snake fence" festooned with old horseshoes. A friend had advised Miss O'Keeffe to put the fence up to keep the rattlesnakes out. The metal fence backed with wire mesh had apparently been effective, because few rattlers had been spotted in recent years. In the distance, the flat-topped volcanic mountain Pedernal was in direct view. Miles of sagebrush and hills stretched between. "Pretty good, isn't it," Miss O'Keeffe remarked simply, referring to her expansive view.

2–3 eggs
1 cup milk
2 tablespoons oil, or
  melted butter
1 cup sifted, unbleached
  flour, or ½ cup sifted,
  unbleached flour and
  ½ cup unsifted, whole
  wheat pastry flour,
  minus 2 tablespoons
½ teaspoon salt

Preheat oven to 450°. Beat together the eggs, milk, and butter or oil, and set them aside. Combine the dry ingredients in a separate bowl, then add the liquid and beat for 2 minutes, until the batter is very smooth. Grease and preheat a muffin pan; fill each cup a little more than ½ full. Bake the popovers at 450° for 20 minutes, then at 350° for 15–20 minutes, or until they are browned and crisp. Serve immediately with butter/oil. Makes 1 dozen popovers.

Miss O'Keeffe had planted several apricot trees around the Abiquiu house. The fruit was usually ripe by mid-July. Many apricots that were not eaten fresh were dried, then frozen for long-term storage. Others were canned or frozen fresh.

The drying process began with washing and drying only unblemished fruit, then halving it and removing the pits. The apricot halves were placed on large screens in wooden frames, then set in the open patio to dry. They were brought into the Indian Room at night. After three or four days in the New Mexico sun, the apricots were dry. They were then packed into plastic bags and stored in the freezer. They could easily be reconstituted and used in muffins, breads, and waffles.

Apricot Muffins

Cover the dried apricots with boiling water. Let them stand at least 30 minutes. During that time, combine the flour, wheat germ, baking powder, salt, and pecans in a large mixing bowl. In a smaller bowl, beat the egg, then add the yogurt, honey, and oil. When the apricots are soft, roughly chop them. Add the wet ingredients and the chopped apricots to the dry ingredients and mix only until slightly blended. Preheat the oven to 400°. Grease a tin for 12 muffins and pour the batter so that each cup is half full. Bake the muffins for 20–25 minutes, or until browned. Serve with butter/oil and fruit preserves, if desired. Makes 1 dozen muffins.

¼ cup dried apricots
Boiling water
1½ cups whole wheat flour
¼ cup raw wheat germ
1 tablespoon baking powder
¼ teaspoon salt
¼ cup pecans, roughly chopped
1 egg
1 cup yogurt
2 tablespoons honey, or to taste
¼ cup oil

Refrigerator Bran Muffins

This is a rare recipe with a commercial product. There were very few boxed or canned brand name items in the O'Keeffe pantry. Miss O'Keeffe enjoyed these with breakfast due to the healthy bran content. Sometimes, breakfast would be brought to the studio or Miss O'Keeffe's bedroom where large glass windows faced south and east. Her bed had been placed very near the windows. Miss O'Keeffe said that this placement made it "almost as if I were right out there in the fields." And at night, the curtains were pulled open so that she could see the moon and the stars.

3 cups bran cereal
½ cup hot water
2 cups buttermilk
2 eggs
¾ cup safflower oil
1 cup brown sugar
1 cup raisins
1½ cups unbleached
    white flour
1 cup whole wheat flour
2 teaspoons baking
    powder
1 teaspoon salt

Preheat the oven to 400°. Combine the bran, water, and buttermilk in a large mixing bowl, and stir well. Let the mixture stand for a few minutes until the cereal absorbs the moisture. Add the eggs, oil, and brown sugar, and beat well. Add the raisins and stir until they are well distributed in the batter. Mix the dry ingredients in a smaller bowl until well blended; add these to the large mixing bowl, stirring only until well combined. Fill greased muffin tins ¾ full, and bake for 15–20 minutes, or until they are lightly browned. Store the remaining batter in a tightly closed container, and place in the refrigerator to use within two weeks. Do not stir the batter again. Serve warm with butter/oil or jam. Makes 36 muffins.

In the fall, as nights grew longer, we might pour over recipes in Prevention magazine—anything from almond soup to skin lotions made with almonds, sunflower seeds, lanolin and almond oil. Miss O'Keeffe was always interested in the benefits of various vitamins and minerals in nuts, seeds, and grains. These muffins have a particularly remarkable variety of nuts which can be adapted to individual tastes.

Atomic Muffins

Preheat the oven to 400°. Chop the almonds, cashews, pecans, and sunflower seeds (or other nuts of choice). Combine the flours, brewer's yeast (if desired), baking powder and salt in a large mixing bowl. In a smaller bowl, beat the egg then add the oil, honey and milk. Add the liquids and nuts to the dry ingredients, and mix until just blended. Grease a muffin tin and fill to ⅔ full. Bake for 15 minutes, or until nicely browned. Serve with butter/oil and fruit preserves. Makes 1 dozen muffins.

¼ cup coarsely chopped almonds
¼ cup coarsely chopped cashew nuts
¼ cup coarsely chopped pecans
¼ cup sunflower seeds
1 cup unbleached white flour
¼ cup soy flour
¾ cup whole wheat flour
2 tablespoons brewer's yeast (optional)
1 tablespoon baking powder
¼ teaspoon salt
1 egg
¼ cup safflower oil
2–3 tablespoons honey
1 cup whole milk

There was an old electric waffle maker on a high shelf in the pantry that was an oddly smaller-than-standard size. It worked well and provided several tasty breakfasts. One early Easter morning, we had waffles by the fire and listened to vocal music by Monteverdi, one of Miss O'Keeffe's favorite records.

Waffles

Approximately ⅔ cup whole wheat flour
1 tablespoon wheat germ
½ teaspoon brewer's yeast (optional)
2 teaspoons baking powder
¼ teaspoon salt
2 tablespoons roughly chopped almonds or pecans
1 egg, separated
¾ cup milk
¼ cup oil
Butter/oil, as a topping
Honey or maple syrup, as a topping

Preheat the waffle iron. When it is hot, grease the top and bottom (if necessary). Mix the dry ingredients in a medium-sized bowl. Separate the egg, and set the egg white aside in a small mixing bowl. Mix the egg yolk, milk, and oil in a small bowl. Add the wet ingredients to the dry and mix them together. Then beat the egg white until stiff peaks form. Fold the egg white into the batter. When the waffle iron "smokes" a little, or when the controls indicate, pour the batter into the waffle iron. After 2–3 minutes, check to see if the waffle is done. When golden brown and crispy, it is ready to eat. Serve with butter/oil and honey or maple syrup.

Miss O'Keeffe felt that buckwheat was a remarkable grain. It does contain a significant amount of protein and magnesium. She frequently referred to a buckwheat pancake recipe that a friend had finally perfected, but then had lost. I developed this recipe to have a balance of different flours, and a lightness due to the buttermilk. As buckwheat is a strong-flavored grain and can be very heavy, it is challenging to cook with. Adjust the amount of buckwheat and wheat flour to taste.

Buckwheat Pancakes

Put the dry ingredients in a large bowl and stir together to blend them. Mix the buttermilk, oil and egg in a smaller bowl. Add the liquid ingredients to the dry ingredients and stir just enough to make the batter fairly smooth. The batter should be somewhat thick but drip easily off a spoon. Allow the batter to sit for three to five minutes. Meanwhile, lightly oil an iron griddle or iron frying pan and heat to just below "smoking"; pour the batter onto the heated surface. Turn the pancakes when they bubble on top, and are moderately brown on one side. Remove from the griddle when the pancakes are browned on both sides. Serve with warmed butter/oil mixture and warmed pure maple syrup. This makes 6–8 medium pancakes.

½ cup buckwheat flour
¼ cup unbleached white flour
¼ cup whole wheat flour
2 teaspoons baking powder
¼ teaspoon salt
2 cups buttermilk or 1½ cups milk
2 tablespoons safflower oil
1 large egg
Butter/oil, as a topping
Warmed maple syrup, as a topping

Millet

Millet is a small, round grain that has a high protein and iron content. Miss O'Keeffe at times requested millet or oatmeal for supper in the winter. She was particular about the fine texture of this grain, so it was pushed through a sieve and reheated. Miss O'Keeffe had specific ideas about the texture, taste, and the proper temperature at which her food should be served. If a bowl or plate for hot food had not been warmed before it was taken to the table, she would remark that the plate was "stone cold."

2 cups water
½ teaspoon salt
1 cup millet
Cream or milk, to taste
Honey, to taste
Apple or banana (optional)

Bring the water and salt to a boil in a small saucepan. Slowly add the millet. Cook it at a low simmer for 15–30 minutes, or until the grain is tender. (Press the millet through a sieve if a finer texture is desired, then reheat.) Serve the cereal in warmed bowls with cream or milk and honey to taste. This cereal is quite good when diced apple and/or banana are added during the last 5 minutes of cooking.

This cereal was a favorite in the winter, for supper rather than for breakfast. Steel-cut oats are quite different in appearance from rolled oats. They contain a high amount of protein and retain more vitamins and minerals than rolled oats; the heat required to process the rolled variety destroys a percentage of their nutritive value.

Oatmeal
(Steel-Cut Oats)

Bring the water and salt to a boil. Add the steel-cut oats and bring to a low simmer for 30–45 minutes, or until the oats are tender. Serve in warmed bowls with cream or milk and honey to taste.

4 cups water
½ teaspoon salt
1 cup steel-cut oats
Cream or milk, to taste
Honey, to taste

There are endless variations to this cereal. Although it contains many calories, the nutritional content is also high due to the whole seeds, nuts, and grains.

Granola

1½ cups sunflower seeds
2 cups coarsely
    chopped or slivered
    almonds with skins
2 cups walnuts, coarsely
    chopped
1 cup cashews, coarsely
    chopped
1 cup raw sesame seeds
1 cup raw wheat germ
6 cups rolled oats
1 cup honey
1 cup safflower oil
2 cups raisins (optional)
2 cups chopped dates
    (optional)
Cream or milk, to taste
Sliced fresh fruit (optional)

Measure the dry ingredients into a very large bowl and stir to mix them. Slowly heat the honey and oil together until the mixture is smooth and runny. Pour the warm liquid over the dry ingredients and stir well to combine the ingredients thoroughly.

Preheat the oven to 350°. Spread the cereal on 2 oiled cookie sheets and place them in the oven. Turn the granola at frequent intervals so that it is lightly browned on all sides. Cool the granola to room temperature, then store it in airtight containers. Serve with cream or milk and sliced fresh fruit, if desired. Makes approximately 4 quarts of granola.

This grain is a flavorful accompaniment to chicken or beef dishes. The ginger imparts a surprising and pleasant flavor to the rice. Miss O'Keeffe enjoyed the strong flavors of garlic, onions, herbs, and ginger. She appreciated individuals who could cook with those ingredients.

In the late 1930s, when Miss O'Keeffe was staying in a large Alcalde ranch house, the female head of the household was a glamorous and very good cook. One summer evening, the painter went to see what the woman was fixing for dinner. She noticed a drip from the roof spilling right into the casserole. Miss O'Keeffe climbed up on the roof and found a big puddle right above the kitchen. It was soon swept off, and the casserole was eaten despite the drips.

Brown Rice with Ginger

Wash the brown rice, then add it to a saucepan with 3 cups of cold water and the salt. When the water boils, reduce the heat to a low simmer and add the ginger. Cook the rice for 30–40 minutes, or until the rice is tender and has absorbed all the water. Do not stir while it is cooking. Serve with butter/oil to taste. Serves 3–4.

1 cup short-grain brown rice
3 cups water
½ teaspoon salt
3 thin slices peeled ginger, chopped coarsely
Butter/oil, to taste

desserts

Desserts were a pleasant ending to many midday and evening meals. Whole grain flours, dairy products, and fruit contributed nutritive components to many of these recipes.

Vanilla Ice Cream

This is a very rich dessert, which we often made in the summer. It is the creamiest ice cream I have ever tasted. On a warm evening after dessert, we might watch the colors change on the Ghost Ranch cliffs. Miss O'Keeffe described how sometimes she had seen it rain so hard that waterfalls poured over the cliffs. "You don't want to be walking near those cliffs if it looks like it's going to rain," she warned. She had walked extensively on the vast Ghost Ranch acreage when it was initially a dude ranch. The land is now owned by the Presbyterian Church (U.S.A), which operates the Ghost Ranch Conference Center on part of its 21,000 acres. Miss O'Keeffe spoke of her joy at walking around the land at night in her nightgown "before the Presbyterians came."

½ cup honey
2 egg yolks
1 teaspoon vanilla
2 pints whipping cream
Fresh raspberries, as a
    topping

In a medium-sized bowl, combine the honey, egg yolks, and vanilla. Set them aside. Whip the 2 pints of cream in a large mixing bowl. Carefully fold the honey-and-egg-yolk mixture into the whipped cream. Set the ice cream mixture in the freezer for 30–45 minutes, or until it begins to freeze. Remove the bowl from the freezer and stir it gently until the mixture again has an even texture. Spoon the ice cream into any preferred storage container and place it in the freezer to harden completely (about 2 hours). Serve the ice cream with fresh raspberries or other fresh fruit.

Several varieties of fruit grew on the Abiquiu grounds. Fruit such as strawberries, cherries, melons, and grapes were bought from Santa Fe markets. Fruit was commonly served with breakfast, as a snack, or as a light dessert. It was dried, canned, or frozen for winter use.

In July and August, we would walk down to the fruit tree terrace to pick ripe apricots and peaches. Another summer treat, although not a fruit, was the abundant rhubarb from the large, healthy plants in the garden.

Stewed Rhubarb

Bring the water and sugar to a boil in a medium saucepan. Add the rhubarb, bring it to a boil, and simmer for 5 minutes. Let the rhubarb cool in the juice. Serve it at room temperature or chilled in individual dessert bowls. This can also be served on top of Vanilla Ice Cream (p. 92). Serves 4.

1 cup water
1 cup sugar
1 pound rhubarb cut into
    ½-inch pieces

Vanilla Rennet Custard

This is a simple, light dessert that we often made. It may be remembered by some as a dish eaten in childhood. Miss O'Keeffe had many memories that she recounted from her childhood days on a sixty-acre Wisconsin farm. She had once used her socks for collecting frogs in post holes left in the ground. She took the frogs back to the house, but was not allowed to bring them inside. She was told she could leave the frogs outside in a big pan. "But of course," she said, "the next morning they were gone."

She enjoyed her mother's reading of *The Leatherstocking Tales* by James Fenimore Cooper and *The Jungle Book* by Rudyard Kipling—and on Sundays she read from the Bible. Miss O'Keeffe commented that she was lucky in the way she had been raised—she could develop in her own way because nobody paid much attention to her.

2 cups whole milk
3 tablespoons sugar
1 teaspoon vanilla
1 tablespoon cold water
1 rennet tablet (Junket ®)

Set aside 4 individual dessert dishes or bowls. Combine the milk, sugar, and vanilla in a small saucepan. Heat the liquid to lukewarm (110°) while stirring. (If the milk gets too hot, cool it to lukewarm.) Put 1 tablespoon of water in a small cup; add the rennet tablet to the water and crush it with a spoon. After the rennet has completely dissolved in the water, pour this into the warm milk and stir for a few seconds only. Quickly pour the liquid into the dishes. Allow the custard to set for 5 minutes, then chill. Serves 4.

Flavored extracts, such as lemon, almond, and orange can be added in place of vanilla. Well-drained fruit can also be placed in the dishes before adding the liquid. To create a creamier texture, replace ½ cup of the milk with cream.

On Miss O'Keeffe's Abiquiu land, she claimed to have "the best applesauce tree around." It bore yellow apples usually in late September. They were picked just before they were ripe, and they made flavorful applesauce.

Two or three varieties of crisp, tart apples were grown on the Abiquiu property. They were carefully wrapped in paper and stored in the cool Indian Room for fall and winter eating. Often, the apples would last until December or January.

When the apples were at their best, they were frequently served fresh, as dessert: apple slices with thin slices of gjetost cheese. Apples were also baked and used in Apple Pie (p. 96) or Norwegian Apple Pie Cake (p. 97).

Applesauce

Wash and quarter the apples. Do not peel or core them. Place the apples in a large kettle with a small amount of water. Simmer them until they are soft. Cool the apples to lukewarm, then press them through a coarse strainer with a pestle, or put them through a food mill. Add sugar to taste and a touch of lemon juice if the apples are not tart enough. Serve warmed, with a pinch of cinnamon. The applesauce can also be frozen or canned.

3 pounds of tart and sweet yellow, red, or green apples
Sugar, to taste
Lemon juice, to taste
Cinnamon

Apple Pie

Occasionally, Miss O'Keeffe attended various Abiquiu events: an anniversary party for old friends, a basketball game in the Abiquiu gym, a wedding in Chimayo. After dessert one evening, she announced that we were going to a rosary in the old Santo Tomás Church in the Abiquiu plaza. We sat toward the back in an old wooden pew. Above us was a small balcony, or gallery, with more pews. "I used to sit in the gallery, but the wood got so creaky, I was afraid it would fall through," she whispered loudly.

1 Whole Wheat Pastry
  Flour Crust (p. 67)
8–10 tart yellow, red, or
  green apples
½ cup sugar
½ teaspoon cinnamon
1 tablespoon butter
1 tablespoon flour
  (optional)
Nutmeg (optional)

Prepare the Whole Wheat Pastry Flour Crust. Divide the dough into 2 balls, one slightly larger than the other. Roll the larger portion out slightly more than ⅛-inch thick, then place it in a 9-inch pie pan.

Quarter and core the apples, and peel them if desired. Cut the quarters into slices no more than ¼-inch thick. Place the apple slices in the pie crust until there is a generous, rounded heap in the center of the pan. Evenly distribute the sugar and cinnamon over the tops of the apples. Dot with 1 tablespoon of butter. (Add 1 tablespoon of flour if the apples are juicy.) Grate a touch of fresh nutmeg over the apples, if desired.

Preheat the oven to 450°. Roll out the other ball of dough to the same thickness as the bottom crust. Place it on top of the apples and pinch the two crusts together along the edge. With a sharp knife, make 3 or 4 short slashes in the top crust. Bake the pie for 10 minutes at 450°, then lower the heat to 350° and bake for 30–40 minutes. If the edge of the crust browns too quickly, cover it with aluminum foil. Serve warm.

During winter suppers, one of Miss O'Keeffe's favorite topics was travel. She had visited Greece, Spain, Italy, Austria, Japan, Nepal, Mexico, and many other countries. She expressed interest in traveling to Australia and Easter Island. Nepal was the only place she said she would like to return to.

Miss O'Keeffe described Hawaii: "The air was lukewarm, as if it were pea soup, and you could hold it in your hand." She told about a man she met in Japan: "He lived by the river and dyed silk; he hung it on branches in the river to rinse, then hung it on the porch to dry." She had a wealth of travel images that were recalled in colorful style.

Norwegian Apple Pie Cake

Preheat the oven to 325°. Combine the sugar and butter in a large mixing bowl. Add the egg and beat until well blended. Next, add the dry ingredients. Mix in the apples and nuts, then stir in the hot water. Bake in a greased 9-inch pie pan for 40 minutes. Serve warm with rum sauce. Serves 6–8.

Compliments of Hilltop Herb Farm, Cleveland, Texas.

1 cup sugar
½ cup butter at room temperature
1 egg
1 cup flour
¼ teaspoon salt
1 teaspoon baking soda
1 teaspoon nutmeg
1 teaspoon cinnamon
2½ cups diced, unpeeled apples
½ cup chopped pecans
2 tablespoons hot water

Rum Sauce

In a small saucepan, combine the brown sugar and cream over low heat. Stir constantly. Add the rum slowly when the cream mixture begins to thicken. This sauce should be the consistency of heavy cream. Drizzle over warm apple pie cake. For added richness, whip ½ cup heavy cream and spoon the whipped cream on top of the cake before drizzling the rum sauce.

½ cup brown sugar
½ cup cream (half and half or heavy cream)
¼ cup rum
½ cup whipped, heavy cream (optional)

Wheat Germ Bars

This was a staple as a dessert, or for an afternoon break, with yogurt or goat's milk. Wheat germ provides complete protein, vitamins E and B, and iron. Cooking destroys some of the vitamin B1 and folic acid, but most of the nutrients remain. Wheat germ was added to many breads and granola to boost their food value.

1 cup brown or raw
   sugar
2 eggs
1 teaspoon vanilla
2 tablespoons oil
¾ cup raw wheat germ
¾ cup pecans

Preheat the oven to 350°. Mix the firmly packed brown sugar and eggs together in a medium-sized bowl. Add the vanilla and oil to this mixture, then add the wheat germ and pecans. Spoon the wheat germ batter into a small, well-oiled baking pan. Bake it for 15–20 minutes, or until it is slightly golden brown. When partially cool, cut it into squares and remove them from the baking pan. Store the squares in an airtight container. Add finely grated orange or lemon peel, chopped almonds, or coconut for taste variety.

This is a traditional northern New Mexico confection. These little cookies are commonly made with white flour; this version with some whole wheat is also quite good. *Biscochitos* are often served during Christmas holidays and with special feasts for weddings, baptisms, and confirmations.

Biscochitos

Cream the sugar and lard or vegetable shortening in a large bowl. Add the 2 eggs and stir until they are well blended. Add the sherry or wine. Add the dry ingredients, 1 cup of flour at a time. Mix well between each added cupful.

Preheat the oven to 350°. Roll the dough out ¼-inch thick on a floured surface. Use a knife or cutter to create a variety of shapes. Sprinkle a mixture of sugar and cinnamon on top of each shape. Bake on greased cookie sheets for 10–12 minutes, or until slightly golden brown.

1 cup sugar
2 cups lard or vegetable shortening
2 eggs
2 tablespoons sherry or wine
1 tablespoon baking powder
1 teaspoon salt
1 teaspoon whole anise seeds
4 cups unbleached white flour
2 cups whole wheat flour
½ teaspoon cinnamon mixed with ¼ cup sugar, to sprinkle on top

Sopaipillas (Buñuelos)

Miss O'Keeffe rarely went out to restaurants, but on one occasion with her visiting family, she graced a nearby establishment. Once the food arrived, everyone seemed pleased with their food except Miss O'Keeffe, who remarked that her *"Platillo Vegetariano"* (Vegetarian Plate) was "entirely indigestible." I inspected her enchilada and discovered they had left out the main ingredient—the cheese. When the puffy fried *"sopaipillas"* arrived, they weren't crisp enough— "rather tired"—according to our gourmet. Of course, the O'Keeffe household made *sopaipillas* that were part whole wheat flour.

1 cup unbleached white flour
1 cup whole wheat flour
2 teaspoons baking powder
¼ teaspoon sea salt
1 tablespoon lard or vegetable shortening
¾ cup water
Vegetable oil for frying
Honey, or cinnamon sugar, as topping

Mix the dry ingredients in a large bowl. Cut the lard or shortening into the flour. Add the water to the dry ingredients, and knead for two minutes. Let the dough sit for ½ hour. Put about 1 inch of oil in a heavy frying pan. Heat the oil until it would make the dough bubble (365°). While the oil is heating, roll the dough out into ⅛-inch triangles or diamonds three inches wide. Slide triangles into the oil from the side of the pan, until they puff and are brown on the bottom; turn to brown on the other side. Let the *sopaipillas* drain on paper towels, and serve warm with honey or cinnamon sugar. Makes 20–25.

This simple fruitcake is a satisfying end to a light supper. It is also very good in thin slices, toasted.

During our meals together, Miss O'Keeffe enjoyed hearing about any particularly interesting or humorous daily events, or about "my young man." After a lengthy discussion about possible marriage, Miss O'Keeffe advised, "My dear, the law makes marriage a very long thing; couldn't you just be tied to him in your heart?"

White Fruit Cake

Preheat the oven to 275°. Grease and flour 3–4 bread pans or 8 small loaf pans. Cream the butter and sugar in a large mixing bowl. Add the eggs one at a time, stirring well between each one. Mix in the dry ingredients, 1 cup of flour at a time. When the batter is smooth, add the lemon extract, raisins, and pecans. Stir well to combine the ingredients evenly. Fill the pans slightly more than half full. Bake the cake until it is golden brown (45 minutes–1 hour) and pulling away from the sides.

Cool the fruitcakes, then store, covered, for 2 days. This allows the fruitcakes to "set"; they are much easier to cut after at least 24 hours. Fruitcakes can be kept almost indefinitely.

2 cups butter at room temperature
2 cups sugar
6 eggs at room temperature
3¼ cups unbleached white flour
1½ teaspoons baking powder
½ teaspoon salt
3 ounces lemon extract
1 pound golden raisins
1 pound whole pecans

Zabaglione

This traditional Italian dessert can be difficult to make "just right." The low heat and slow addition of the wine are the keys to successful zabaglione. The liquid will become thick and foamy very quickly after all the alcohol has been added if the heat is appropriately low.

After dessert on dark winter evenings, Miss O'Keeffe and I would walk back to her studio and attempt to keep up with current events by reading *Time*, *Smithsonian*, *National Geographic*, or sections from the *New York Times* bold print edition. Her favorite topics were travel, politics, the environment, and art. At one time, we brought a small television into the kitchen so that we could watch the six o'clock news. The main distraction, however, was the advertisements. "What you have to go through to get the news!" she remarked. She soon chose to return to the reading method for getting the news.

3 egg yolks
2 tablespoons sugar
⅓ cup marsala, port, or sherry
Freshly grated nutmeg, as garnish

Heat water to barely simmering in the bottom of a double boiler. Separate the 3 eggs and put the egg yolks in the top of the double boiler, off the heat. Add the sugar to the egg yolks and beat them until they are thick and lemon-colored. Set the egg yolk and sugar mixture above the simmering water and beat constantly with a rotary or electric beater. Add the wine very slowly, continuing to beat the mixture until it is smooth, light, and holds its shape. (If it is beaten too long, it will become heavy and runny.) Spoon into individual dessert cups or glasses. A pinch of freshly grated nutmeg can be added on top. Commercially made Lady Fingers cookies are a traditional accompaniment to this dish. Serve while warm or chill. Serves 3.

beverages

Miss O'Keeffe enjoyed a variety of beverages: from yogurt, juices, and teas, to coffee and beer or wine in moderation. Fresh orange and carrot juices were favorites. Yogurt was routinely served for a mid-morning or mid-afternoon break from the day's activities. Miss O'Keeffe considered it to be a healthful household necessity. Another valued dairy product was goat's milk. At one time, neighbors across the Chama River developed a goat dairy. Miss O'Keeffe frequently requested this milk since the animals had not been given drugs or chemicals. Referring to most commercially produced milk, she commented, "Our milk these days is terribly abused."

Miss O'Keeffe usually woke up three or four times during the night. She always requested some type of fruit and yogurt or goat's milk for her awake periods. Often while she was awake she listened to recorded versions of magazines, such as *Time* or *U.S. News and World Report,* or specific recorded books. I slept in a bedroom next to hers and, at times, would awaken to portions of *Stalking the Wilderness* or the *Tao Te Ching.* Talking books were checked out from the State Library for the Blind, as Miss O'Keeffe's eyes were not sharp enough for reading. Referring to this service, she remarked, "It's the one thing that the government does for the people."

Fresh Carrot Juice

Early spring was a joy to be in the garden and survey the first plants. Near the end of April, chives, parsley, mint, sorrel, and lovage were appearing. The jonquils were sending up their shoots as well, and bees were buzzing in the blossoming trees. By May, Miss O'Keeffe and the gardener could gather great limbs of lilacs to put in one special, very large vase. The last frost date is May 25 in northern New Mexico. Near that date, seeds and seedlings were planted in great anticipation of the coming garden season. What is a sweeter treat than a young garden carrot?

Carrot juice was enjoyed in the summer, mid-morning or mid-afternoon. If the garden's supply of carrots was too small, large bags of organic carrots were purchased in Santa Fe at the health food store or food co-op.

8 to 10 organic carrots
Electric juicer

Scrub the carrots well until they are clean. Cut off only the very tops and any undesired sections at the tips. Peel the carrots if you prefer. If necessary, cut any large sections in two pieces in order to fit into the juicer. Place a glass under the juicer spout. Turn on the juicer and push the carrot segments into the mouth of the juicer with the provided stopper. Turn off the juicer when all the carrots have gone through. This makes two small glasses of juice.

Yogurt

If you are using the powdered yogurt starter, follow directions on the package. If using prepared yogurt, pour the milk into a large saucepan and slowly heat it to lukewarm (110°). When the milk is the correct temperature, remove ½ cup and mix it with the yogurt. Stir them together until they are smooth, then add this cup of liquid to the milk in the saucepan. Stir until it is smooth. Pour the milk and yogurt mixture into glass jars, up to ½ inch below the rim. Put the jars in an electric yogurt maker for 4–6 hours or set the jars in warm water (100°–120°) and maintain the temperature for 4–6 hours. When the yogurt thickens, cover, and store it in the refrigerator.

Most often, yogurt was served plain. Sometimes half of a banana was blended into the yogurt with a pinch of cinnamon. This yogurt is also very good with sliced fresh peaches, pears, or apricots.

Powdered yogurt starter, or ¼ cup high-quality yogurt
½ gallon whole cow's milk or goat's milk
4 1-pint glass canning jars, sterilized
Electric yogurt maker, or large pan containing warm water

Goat's Milk

Late one Saturday morning, my telephone rang and Miss O'Keeffe called to announce with great pleasure that she had just finished a new painting. "But I just washed my hair and my head is all wet," I said. "You can dry it here in my bathroom." She easily persuaded me to come and view the latest in her abstract series "From a Day with Juan," while she in her painter's smock, ate homemade cookies and fresh goat's milk.

Fresh goat's milk, from certified goat farmers' dairies

Goat's milk can be drunk fresh, or used in yogurt or in any recipes which call for milk. The molecular structure of goat's milk is the same as that of human milk.

We made this tea year-round, as a quantity of mint was dried every fall. Generally, it was served after the noon meal and after supper—from a small, white Japanese teapot with a straw handle into little white cups.

Spearmint is known as *yerbabuena* or "good herb" in New Mexico. It has long been known to soothe the stomach and to aid the digestive process. Three different types of mint were grown in the Abiquiu garden. We most often chose spearmint, as it had the strongest, most pleasing flavor.

Mint Tea

Cut the fresh mint sprigs, including only healthy green leaves. Wash them and set them aside. When the water boils, pour a small amount into the teapot to warm it. Discard that water, then put the fresh mint sprigs or dried leaves into the pot. Pour boiling water over the mint and fill the teapot. Let the tea steep for 5 minutes or more. Serve hot or pour over ice cubes for iced tea. A touch of sugar or honey may be preferred in this tea.

8 or 9 long sprigs of fresh mint leaves, or ¼ to ⅓ cup of dried mint leaves
1 quart of boiling water
Sugar or honey, to taste

Fenugreek Tea

Fenugreek is one of the world's oldest medicinal plants. It was used by the ancient Egyptians and Greeks. This tea is recommended for a variety of benefits from the treatment of fevers and sore throats to the cleansing of the digestive system. For several months, we cultivated the habit of drinking fenugreek tea after supper. We became accustomed to its mild, somewhat maple flavor. Miss O'Keeffe commented that if we drank this tea regularly, we would become "as pure as the driven snow."

1 teaspoon fenugreek tea per 6 ounce cup of tea
1 quart boiling water

When the water boils, pour a small amount into the teapot to heat it. Discard this water, then measure the desired amount of fenugreek seeds into the pot. Pour the boiling water over the seeds and steep for 5 minutes or more. The exterior of the fenugreek seeds will become gelatinous and will clump in the bottom of the teapot; conveniently, the seeds do not pour out into the cups. Fenugreek makes a pale green tea with a rather sweet and slightly nutlike taste.

Yarrow is a hardy perennial that grows in many areas of the United States. The tea has a history of use for stomach and other internal pains and for aiding colds and coughs. This tea is very effective is soothing sore throats and coughs. The following recipe is adapted from *Prevention,* a health-oriented magazine that has been in circulation since 1950. Miss O'Keeffe was quite interested in the contents of this publication, which focus on exercise, weight control, nutrition, food preparation, medical treatment, and personal care.

Yarrow Tea

When the water boils, pour some into the pot to warm it. Then discard the water. Measure 1 teaspoon of yarrow for each cup of tea. The dried yarrow can be put directly into the pot or measured into a tea infuser. Pour the desired amount of boiling water over the yarrow. Add honey to taste, 1 teaspoon of lemon juice per cup, and up to ⅛ teaspoon of cayenne pepper per pot of tea. The pepper makes this a very spicy tea. However, the cayenne and yarrow have cleansing properties, which effectively soothe a sore throat and cough.

Dried yarrow flowers
Honey, to taste
1 teaspoon fresh lemon
    juice
Cayenne pepper, to
    taste
1 quart boiling water

Front cover: *O'Keeffe Making a Stew at the Ghost Ranch* 1961. Photograph © Todd Webb, Courtesy of Estate of Todd Webb, Portland, Maine.

Museum of New Mexico Press edition
© 2009 by Margaret Wood

Cover design by Bette Brodsky
Interior design based on original design by Beverly Miller Atwater
Manufactured in the United States
Museum of New Mexico Press edition:
10 9 8 7

Library of Congress Cataloging-in-Publication Data
Wood, Margaret, 1953-
    A Painter's Kitchen: recipes from the kitchen of Georgia O'Keeffe / by Margaret Wood. — 2nd ed.
        p.   cm.
Includes index
ISBN 978-089013-560-0
1. cookery, american. 2. Painters—New Mexico. I. O'Keeffe, Georgia, 1887–1986.
II. Title.
TX715.W8826   1997
641.5973-dc21

Museum of New Mexico Press
Post Office Box 2087
Santa Fe, New Mexico 87504
www.mnmpress.org